A Concise
Introduct...

ALSO AVAILABLE

A Concise Introduction to Ami Pro 3

by

P.R.M. Oliver
and
N. Kantaris

BERNARD BABANI (publishing) LTD.
THE GRAMPIANS
SHEPHERDS BUSH ROAD
LONDON W6 7NF
ENGLAND

PLEASE NOTE

Although every care has been taken with the production of this book to ensure that any projects, designs, modifications and/or programs, etc., contained herewith, operate in a correct and safe manner and also that any components specified are normally available in Great Britain, the Publishers and Author(s) do not accept responsibility in any way for the failure (including fault in design) of any project, design, modification or program to work correctly or to cause damage to any equipment that it may be connected to or used in conjunction with, or in respect of any other damage or injury that may be so caused, nor do the Publishers accept responsibility in any way for the failure to obtain specified components.

Notice is also given that if equipment that is still under warranty is modified in any way or used or connected with home-built equipment then that warranty may be void.

© 1993 and 1995 BERNARD BABANI (publishing) LTD

First Published - February 1993
Revised Edition - January 1995

British Library Cataloguing in Publication Data:

Oliver, P.R.M.
    Concise Introduction To Ami Pro 3
    I. Title II. Kantaris N.
    652.55369

    ISBN 0 85934 306 5

Printed and Bound in Great Britain by Cox & Wyman Ltd, Reading

ABOUT THIS BOOK

A Concise Introduction To Ami Pro 3 has been written for those who want to get to grips with the Lotus Ami Pro Windows word processor and desk top publishing package in the fastest possible time. No previous knowledge is assumed, but it does not describe how to set up your computer hardware, or how to install Microsoft Windows. If you need to know more about these topics, then may we suggest that you also refer to one of the books *A Concise User's Guide to MS-DOS 5* (BP318), *MS-DOS 6 Explained* (BP341), or *A Concise User's Guide to Windows 3.1* (BP325). All these books are also published by BERNARD BABANI (publishing) LTD

This book was written with the busy person in mind. It is not necessary to read seven or eight hundred pages covering all there is to know about a subject, when a few selected concise pages can do the same thing quite adequately, and much more cheaply! With the help of this book, it is hoped that you will be able to get the most out of Ami Pro 3 and your computer in terms of efficiency, productivity and enjoyment, and that you will be able to do it in the shortest, most effective and informative way.

More emphasis has been placed on an understanding of what we consider to be the critical areas in the program, such as page layout, paragraph styles and the use of frames, than on a general overall description of the package. Although we have tried to make the book as complete as possible.

This second edition of the book has been fully revised and laid out using the **Ami Pro 3.1** program and very few problems were encountered. We have always liked the Ami Pro package, and feel that it stands comparison with anything else in the marketplace.

The version of the program we used was included as part of Lotus SmartSuite 3.0, but the book is equally applicable to the stand alone version of Ami Pro 3. Most of the screen dump illustrations do however show the SmartCenter bar of icons.

None of the new features included in version 3.1 were documented in the printed manuals that came with the package. If you need this information, it is included in the file

README31.SAM which is installed by default with other sample Ami Pro documents in the directory \amipro\docs. It is an easy matter to print this file. In fact many of the improvements are concerned with program and document sharing and interaction over a network, which are beyond the scope of this book.

We have included new sections to introduce the Equation editor and Revision Marking, both are features well worth researching.

Many of the extras included with 3.1 are in the form of macros, most of which can be accessed from SmartIcons. We recommend you explore these when you have worked through the basics of the program and we have included brief details of them in an Appendix.

If you would like to purchase a floppy disc containing all the files which appear in this, or any other listed book(s) by the same author(s), then fill-in the form at the back of the book and send it to P. R. M. Oliver at the stipulated address.

ABOUT THE AUTHORS

Phil Oliver graduated in Mining Engineering at Camborne School of Mines in 1967 and since then has specialised in most aspects of surface mining technology, with a particular emphasis on computer related techniques. He has worked in Guyana, Canada, several Middle Eastern countries, South Africa and the United Kingdom, on such diverse projects as: the planning and management of bauxite, iron, gold and coal mines; rock excavation contracting in the UK; international mining equipment sales and technical back up and international mine consulting for a major mining house in South Africa. In 1988 he took up a lecturing position at Camborne School of Mines (part of Exeter University) in Surface Mining and Management.

Noel Kantaris graduated in Electrical Engineering at Bristol University and after spending three years in the Electronics Industry in London, took up a Tutorship in Physics at the University of Queensland. Research interests in Ionospheric Physics, led to the degrees of M.E. in Electronics and Ph.D. in Physics. On return to the UK, he took up a Post-Doctoral Research Fellowship in Radio Physics at the University of Leicester, and then in 1973 a lecturing position in Engineering at the Camborne School of Mines, Cornwall, (part of Exeter University), where since 1978 he has also assumed the responsibility for the Computing Department.

ACKNOWLEDGEMENTS

We would like to thank the staff of Lotus Development UK for the provision of software for the preparation of this book. We would also like to thank colleagues at the Camborne School of Mines for the helpful tips and suggestions which assisted us in the writing of this book.

TRADEMARKS

CONTENTS

1. PACKAGE OVERVIEW

Ami Pro has the distinction of being the only fully fledged word processor that has been designed, from its inception, for the Microsoft Windows environment; whereas its major contenders have been adapted to work with Windows from previous text based DOS versions. In all its versions Ami Pro has had a heavy bias towards desk top publishing and Version 3 offers fully editable WYSIWYG (what you see is what you get) modes that can be viewed in various zoom levels, including full page. Couple this with the ability to include and manipulate full colour graphics and you can see that the program has enormous power. Once you have overcome the first hurdle and started to use Ami Pro for your word processing you will find it both intuitive and easy to produce the type of output you would not have dreamt possible before.

Ami Pro 3.1, which is packaged with Lotus SmartSuite 3 requires that you have version 3.1 of Windows running on your computer.

New Features
Some of the major enhancements Ami Pro 3.0 had over earlier releases of the package include:

- The ability to 'drag and drop' text when editing text and tables in documents, this is more convenient than cutting and pasting.
- A fast format feature to copy the format of selected text to any other text in a document.
- A clean screen option which removes, at a stroke, the frames and borders, etc., from the screen. This gives a larger working area and will appeal to previous WordPerfect users.
- A grammar checker with settings for casual, business or technical writing.
- A redesigned SmartIcon system, including an icon editor.
- Preview facilities for Style Sheets, and ability to browse files before opening them.

1

- Automated printing of envelopes and labels.
- The new SmartMerge step-by-step guide to the merge function.
- An on-line tutorial.
- A WordPerfect Switchkit to ease the change from that word processor.

Other Features
Some of the other enhancements and features to be found in all versions of Ami Pro 3 include:

- Transparent importing of existing files produced by almost all other main word processors.
- Outlining with click-and-drag facility.
- Extensive spell checker and thesaurus.
- Equation generator with maths and Greek characters.
- Comprehensive table facility which automatically formats text or numbers in cells.
- Master document command to compile books, as well as Index, Table of Contents and Table of Authorities generation.
- A much enhanced context sensitive Help command.
- The use of Frames for placing and overlaying text and/or graphics.
- Automatic built-in charting with 3D or perspective options.
- Complex freehand drawing tools including Bezier curves, lines, boxes, arrows and image and text rotation.
- A library of 100 clip-art drawings.
- Import facilities for the major graphic formats and the ability to edit Lotus and Windows produced graphic files.

Ami Pro version 3.1 includes several new file import and export filters and adds the following new features:

- Document Sharing Application - network access to a special Lotus Notes database.
- Send Mail Memo - allows you to send mail messages through Lotus Notes and Lotus cc:Mail.

- Allows you to specify continuations for any footnote text that does not fit on one page.
- Lets you display the 'Welcome to Ami Pro' dialogue box each time you start the program.

SmartIcons:

These are now an important part of all the Windows application software produced by Lotus. They are colourful buttons, or speed-keys, that give you mouse click access to the functions most often used in the program.

Where feasible, SmartIcons are standard across the Lotus applications which makes their learning and use much easier. The usual drop menus are still present but are only necessary now for the lesser used commands. In Ami Pro 3 there are different sets of SmartIcons for each type of work being carried out. It is an easy matter to connect your own macros to customised icon buttons and make up your own sets. You can locate SmartIcon bars anywhere on the screen and if you right-mouse-click on one, a description of its function is flashed on the screen. All in all, SmartIcons make using Ami Pro much easier and far more fun.

Style Sheets:

Ami Pro differs in one basic way from DOS based word processors in that it uses style sheets to control the formatting of pages and paragraphs within a document. Once you get accustomed to this it saves you an enormous amount of time with document formatting. Over 50 pre-defined style sheets are provided with the package. These alone should allow you to create attractive and functional letters, memos, reports, books, etc., but you can also modify these in any way you like to make completely new styles for your documents. This book was written with Ami Pro 3.1 using a customised style sheet which produced camera ready pages for the printers.

Style sheets can include text and graphics in which case they can be previewed from a list before being selected. Some of the provided sheets are automated and prompt you for the information needed to create a document. The Style Sheet Guide provided with the package gives details of the standard styles you can use. These include a basic one, three for calendars, and several for expense account layouts, envelopes, faxes, letters, indexes, contents pages, labels, invoices, memos, newsletters, outlines, overheads, lists, reports and title pages. A very comprehensive list indeed.

Hardware Requirements

You can install Ami Pro 3.0 on an IBM AT compatible or PS/2 computer equipped with an 80286 or higher processor, at least 4MB of RAM and with Microsoft Windows 3.1 installed. We would not recommend this however for version 3.1, SmartSuite requires at least a 386 based PC with VGA screen and a mouse. Installing the complete version of Ami Pro 3.1 on such a machine requires about 16.5MB of hard disc space. A mouse is a must if you are going to benefit from the program's features and from Window's Graphical User Interface (GUI).

If you install the whole of Lotus SmartSuite 3 you will require at least 93MB of hard disc space! It's a good job the price of large capacity disc drives has dropped considerably over the last few years.

Installing Ami Pro

Installing Ami Pro 3.1 on your computer's hard disc is made very easy with the use of the INSTALL program, either on Disk 1 of the SmartSuite set, or of the individual program set. You need to run this program because part of its job is to convert compressed files from the distribution discs prior to copying them onto your hard disc; it then configures Windows for Ami Pro and any other packages loaded. As most people will probably load Ami as part of the Lotus SmartSuite we will briefly describe that procedure.

Insert the distribution disc #1 into drive A: and start the installation from the Program Manager of Windows, by clicking your mouse on **File**, followed by **Run** and typing

```
A:\Install
```

in the dialogue box. The first time you do this you will be asked to type your name on one of the initial screens produced. This is a type of software copy protection, but Ami

Pro will also use the information to generate a set of initials for you which may be used later, if you carry out document correcting for example. If you are installing over a previous version of SmartSuite the original details will be offered. When this authentication operation is complete, a screen similar to the following should be displayed:

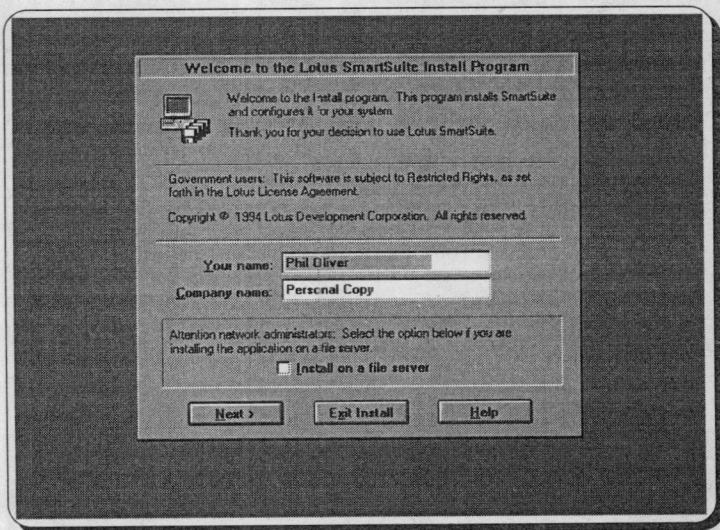

Welcome to the Lotus SmartSuite Install Program

Welcome to the Install program. This program installs SmartSuite and configures it for your system.

Thank you for your decision to use Lotus SmartSuite.

Government users: This software is subject to Restricted Rights, as set forth in the Lotus License Agreement.

Copyright © 1994 Lotus Development Corporation. All rights reserved.

Your name: Phil Oliver
Company name: Personal Copy

Attention network administrators: Select the option below if you are installing the application on a file server.

☐ Install on a file server

Next >   Exit Install   Help

You have now started a long and drawn-out procedure, so we hope you have made yourself a cup of coffee and are sitting very comfortably.

If the details of **Your name** and your **Company name** are correct, click your mouse on the **Next** button to proceed. In most of the dialogue boxes you can use the **Help** button to get more details of the installation procedure expected. If all else fails the **Exit Install** button will let you 'bail out' and try again later.

We will assume that if you are attempting to **Install on a file server** (in other words for an installation to be used across a network) you will not be using this book as a guide!

The **Next** button opens the following box from which you select drive and directory details for the main installation.

5

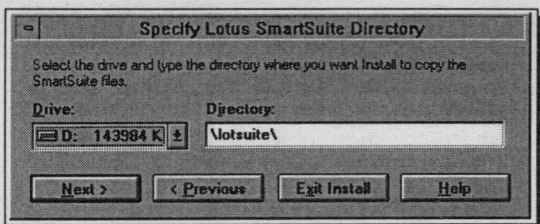

Specify Lotus SmartSuite Directory

Select the drive and type the directory where you want Install to copy the SmartSuite files.

Drive:
D: 143984 K

Directory:
\lotsuite\

Next >   < Previous   Exit Install   Help

From now on you also have the option of going back one step by pressing the **Previous** button.

From the **Next** box you select which of the SmartSuite programs you want to install.

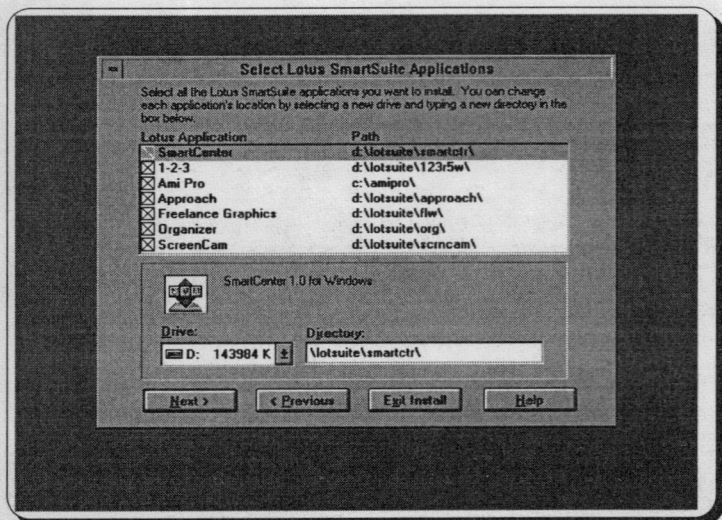

Select Lotus SmartSuite Applications

Select all the Lotus SmartSuite applications you want to install. You can change each application's location by selecting a new drive and typing a new directory in the box below.

Lotus Application	Path
SmartCenter	d:\lotsuite\smartctr\
1-2-3	d:\lotsuite\123r5w\
Ami Pro	c:\amipro\
Approach	d:\lotsuite\approach\
Freelance Graphics	d:\lotsuite\flw\
Organizer	d:\lotsuite\org\
ScreenCam	d:\lotsuite\scrncam\

SmartCenter 1.0 for Windows

Drive:
D: 143984 K

Directory:
\lotsuite\smartctr\

Next >   < Previous   Exit Install   Help

The default selection is to install everything, as shown above. You also have the option of changing the drive and directory for the programs you want. We have chosen above to place Ami Pro in the directory C:\Amipro, but all the other programs on our D: drive.

When you have selected what programs to install you will be given the option of customising your installation in the box shown on the facing page.

```
┌─┬─────────────────────────────────────────────────┐
│ ─ │              Install Options                     │
├───┴─────────────────────────────────────────────────┤
│ Select the features you want to install.             │
│ ┌─ Install options ─────────────────────────────────┐│
│ │ ⦿ Default features - Automatic install            ││
│ │   Automatically installs the typical features of each application in ││
│ │   SmartSuite.                                      ││
│ │                                                    ││
│ │ ○ Minimum features - Automatic install            ││
│ │   Automatically installs only the minimum features needed to run each ││
│ │   application in SmartSuite. Use this option for laptops with limited disk ││
│ │   space                                            ││
│ │                                                    ││
│ │ ○ Customize features - Manual install             ││
│ │   You decide for each application whether you install all features, the ││
│ │   minimum features, or only the specific features you select.  ││
│ └────────────────────────────────────────────────────┘│
│ ┌─────────┐ ┌──────────┐ ┌────────────┐ ┌──────────┐ │
│ │ Next >  │ │ < Previous│ │ Exit Install│ │  Help    │ │
│ └─────────┘ └──────────┘ └────────────┘ └──────────┘ │
└─────────────────────────────────────────────────────┘
```

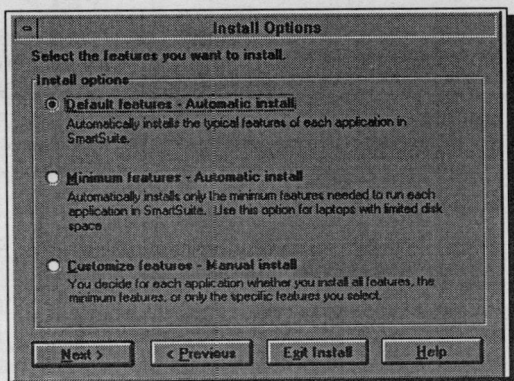

If you have enough space on your hard disk we suggest you choose the **Default features - Automatic install** option, if not you will have to either install the **Minimum features** option (suitable for a laptop), or use the **Customize features - Manual install** option, to include any other features that you have room for. For our purposes we will assume you are carrying out a complete installation, so select the default.

Selecting **Yes** from the next box should now start the process of copying the files from up to 30 high density discs to your hard disc drive. As the installation proceeds a series of info screens, like that below, give details of some of the Suite features. These screens are decorative and informative and should prevent you getting too bored.

Lotus SMARTSUITE

The Complete Solution for Windows desktops

Five top-of-the-line applications – 1-2-3, Ami Pro, Approach, Freelance Graphics, and Organizer— make SmartSuite 3.0 the only complete solution for Windows desktops.

With Organizer and Approach, SmartSuite is also the only desktop suite that provides tools for managing schedules, maintaining lists, and creating your own reports.

If the complete SmartSuite package is installed 30 high density distribution disks will be used. The program then adds 21 icons to the 'Lotus Applications' Icon Group of the Windows Program manager, as shown below (unless, that is, you asked for them to be placed in one of your other groups). With luck your installation should now be complete and you will have much exploring to do.

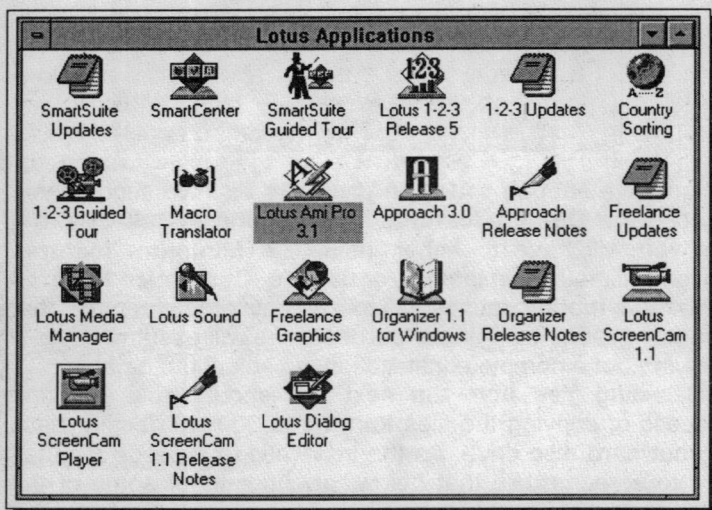

2. THE AMI PRO ENVIRONMENT

Starting the Program

You can start Ami Pro from the DOS prompt by specifying the complete program path, which in our case, would be:

```
win C:\AMIPRO\amipro
```

Ami Pro Program Icon:

It is more usual however to start the program when Windows is already running, by either double clicking the left mouse button on the Ami Pro icon shown here, or by double clicking on an Ami document file (with the extension .SAM) in the Windows File Manager. In this case the document will be loaded into Ami Pro at the same time.

If you have Lotus Smartsuite 3 active on your PC, you can also start Ami Pro by clicking the SmartCenter icon shown here. This set of icons will be displayed whenever you are in Windows.

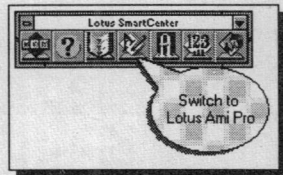

The Welcome Screen:

The first time Ami Pro 3.1 is opened the Welcome box shown below should be opened. The option to **Create a new document** is the default, which will be actioned when you select **OK.** The alternative is to **Work on an existing document**.

To prevent this box showing whenever you enter Ami Pro, you can mark the **Don't show this screen again** option. To remove it from the screen for this time only, select **Cancel**.

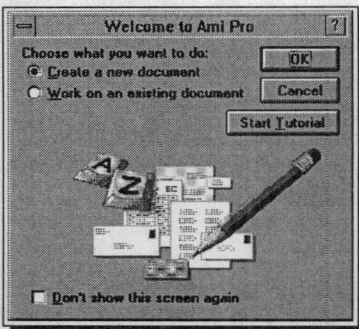

9

QuickStart Tutorial:

Clicking the **Start Tutorial** button in the 'Welcome to Ami Pro' box will open the QuickStart Tutorial as shown below. This tutorial is a good introduction to the powerful features of Ami Pro. It takes about 30 minutes to work through and is well worth the time.

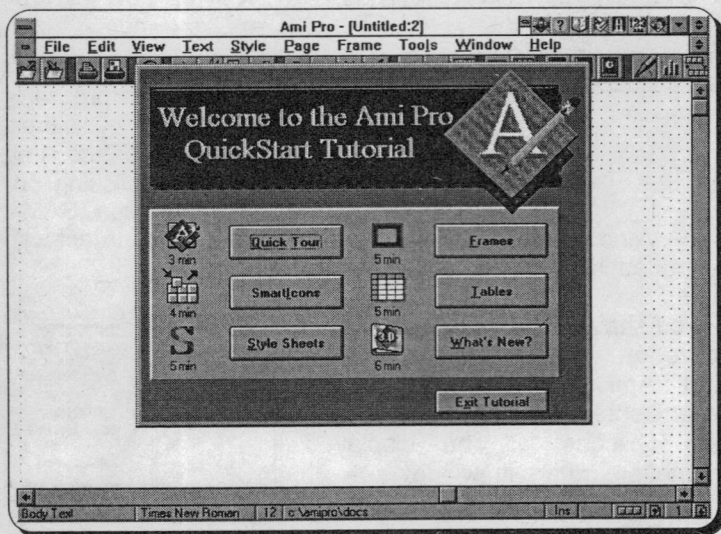

Be patient in the tutorial, you will not have control of the cursor and it sometimes seems to take forever to move across the screen. You can of course run through the process as often as you like. When you have finished with the tutorial you can return to the main Ami Pro screen from the QuickStart Menu with the **Exit Tutorial** button. To abandon a section of the tutorial, press the <Esc> key and click on the **QuickStart Menu** button. If you need to run the tutorial again at any stage in the future, simply click on the **Help** menu, followed by the **QuickStart Tutorial**.

The Ami Pro Screen

The opening 'blank' screen of Ami Pro 3 is shown on the facing page. It is perhaps worth spending some time looking at the various parts that make up this screen, or window. Ami follows the usual Microsoft Windows conventions and if you are familiar with these you can skip through this section. Otherwise a few minutes might be well spent here.

The window as shown takes up the full screen area available. If you click on the application restore button, the top one of the two restore buttons at the top right of the screen, you can make Ami show in a smaller window. This can be useful when you are running several applications at the same time and you want to transfer between them with the mouse.

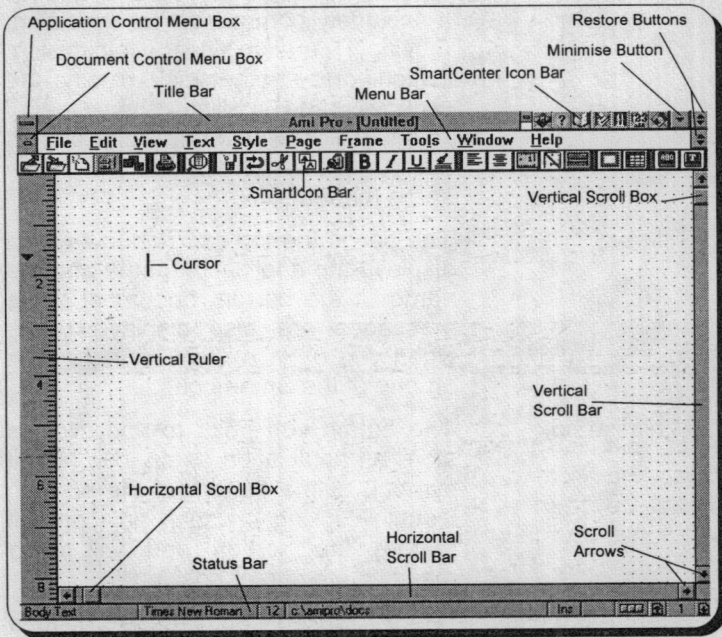

Note that the Ami window, which in this case displays an empty (and [Untitled]) document, has a solid 'Title bar', indicating that it is the active application window. Although multiple windows can be displayed simultaneously, you can only enter data into the active window (which will always be displayed on top). Title bars of non active windows appear a lighter shade than that of the active one.

The Ami Pro screen is divided into several areas which have the following functions. These are described from the top of the screen down, working from left to right.

Area	*Function*
Control boxes	Clicking on the top control menu box, which is located in the upper left corner of the window, displays the pull-down Control menu which can be used to control the program window. It includes commands for re-sizing, moving, maximising, minimising, switching to another task, closing the window, and calling the Control Panel. The lower menu box controls the current document window in the same manner.
Title bar	The bar at the top of a window which displays the application name and the name of the current document. Help messages are also displayed here when you open a menu or right click on one of the SmartIcons.
Minimise box	The button you point to and click to store an application as an icon (small symbol) at the bottom of the screen. Double clicking on such an icon will restore the screen and will even maintain the cursor position.
Restore buttons	When clicked on, these buttons restore the active window to the position and size occupied before being maximised or minimised. The restore button is then replaced by a Maximise button, with a single up-pointing arrow, which can be used to set the window to its former size.

Menu bar	The bar below the title bar which allows you to choose from several menu options. Clicking on a menu item displays the pull-down menu associated with that item.
SmartIcons	Displays the current set of icons, which can be clicked on to quickly carry out commands, functions or macros.
Scroll bars	The areas on the screen (extreme right and bottom of each window) that contain scroll boxes in vertical and horizontal bars. Clicking on these bars allows you to control the part of a document which is visible on the screen.
Scroll arrows	The arrowheads at each end of each scroll bar at which you can click to scroll the screen up and down one line, or left and right 10% of the screen, at a time.
Status bar	The bottom line of the screen that displays a series of Ami shortcut buttons, as well as program information.

The Menu Bar Options:

Each menu bar option has associated with it a pull-down sub-menu. To activate the menu, either press the <Alt> key, which causes the first option of the menu (in this case the Document Control Menu box) to be highlighted, then use the right and left arrow keys to highlight any of the options in the menu, or use the mouse to point to an option. Pressing either the <Enter> key, or the left mouse button, reveals the pull-down sub-menu of the highlighted menu option. The sub-menu of the **File** option is shown overleaf:

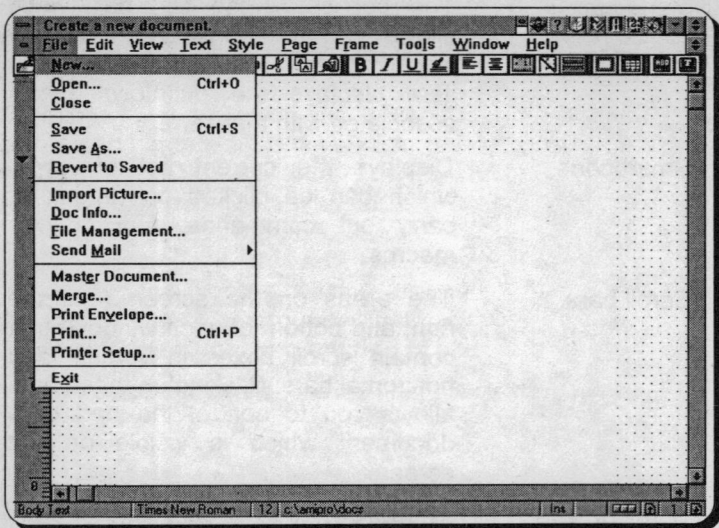

Menu options can also be activated directly by pressing the
<Alt> key followed by the underlined letter of the required
option. Thus, pressing **Alt+F**, causes the pull-down **File**
sub-menu to be displayed. You can use the up and down
arrow keys to move the highlighted bar up and down a
sub-menu, or the right and left arrow keys to move along the
options in the menu bar. Note that as you move up and down
a sub-menu the title line shows a brief description of the
highlighted option. Pressing the <Enter> key selects the
highlighted option or executes the highlighted command.
Pressing the <Esc> key once, closes the pull-down
sub-menu, while pressing the <Esc> key for a second time,
closes the menu system.

Some of the sub-menu options can be accessed with
'quick key' combinations from the keyboard. Such
combinations are shown on the drop down menus, for
example, <Ctrl+S> is the quick key for the **Save** option in the
File sub-menu. If a sub-menu option is not available, at any
time, it will display in a grey colour. Some menu options only
appear in Ami Pro when that tool is being used, but the
following options remain constant.

14

For a more detailed description of each sub-menu item, either highlight it and read the text on the title line, or use the on-line **Help** system, described later.

File   Produces a pull-down menu of mainly file related tasks, such as creating a **New** document, the ability to **Open**, or **Close** files, and **Save** files with the same name, or **Save As** a different name. Options to **Import Pictures** into documents, manage other files and long 'book type' projects, to **Save Mail**, set-up and use **Print**ers and finally to **Exit** the program, are included.

Edit   This menu gives options to **Undo** changes made, to move, delete and copy text and graphics, to **Find & Replace** text, to jump to any location in a document, to **Insert** notes, bullets, the time and/or the date, objects, **Power Fields**, etc., and to **Mark Text** and add **Bookmarks**.

View   This menu gives screen display options and is split into four sections. You can choose to display one or two pages, or part of a page at a chosen size. You can choose between draft, outline or full WYSIWYG modes. The remaining options determine what features, if any, you want on your working screen.

Text   This sub-menu allows you to alter the appearance of text, both on the screen and when printed. Such features as font, size, colour, alignment, print spacing, justification, case and enhancements (bold, underlined and italic) are included along with a **Fast Format** option to allow you to copy any of these text formats from one section of text to another in one operation.

Style   Allows you to **Define**, **Create**, **Select** and **Modify** paragraph styles, as well as to

	Save, **Use** and generally **Manage** style sheets.

Page Produces a sub-menu to control how your document pages will look, including **Headers, Footers**, to set and change page size and layout, show a ruler on the screen, also to set **Page** and **Line Numbering** and **Breaks** options.

Frame The **Frame** sub-menu has options for creating and modifying frames (much more on this later in the book), for scaling graphic images within a frame and for manipulating groups of frames.

Tools Gives access to the **Spell** and **Grammar Checker**s, the **Thesaurus**, **Table** manipulation, **Drawing** tools, **Chart** and **Equation** generators, some advanced document building and editing tools, **SmartIcon** control and building tools, **User Setup** screens and a **Macro** generator and playback facility.

Window Produces a sub-menu to open a **New Window**, and control the display of existing open windows on the screen.

Help Activates the help window and displays an 'index' of help or offers help on selected topics; as well as giving access to the **QuickStart Tutorial**, over 500 pages on **Macro** Documentation.

Dialogue Boxes:

Three periods after a sub-menu option or command, means that a dialogue box will open when the option or command is selected. A dialogue box is used for the insertion of additional information, such as the name of a file or path.

To see a dialogue box, press **Alt+F**, and select the **Open** option. The 'File Open' dialogue box appears on the screen and should look similar to the following:

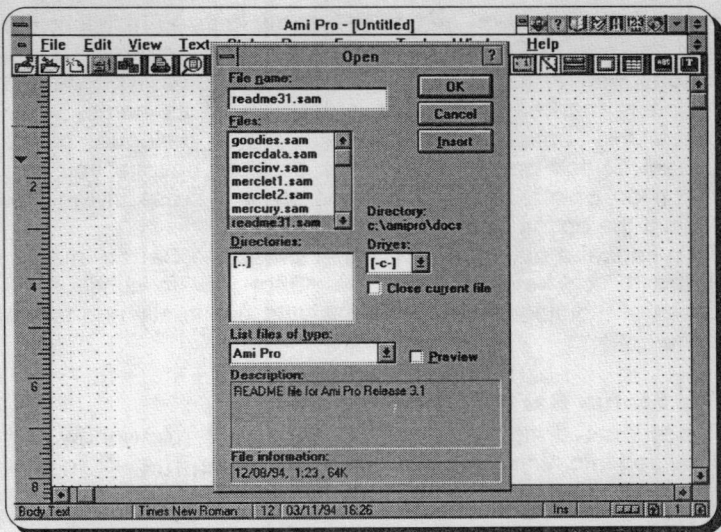

When a dialogue box opens, the easiest way to move around it is by clicking with the mouse, otherwise the <Tab> key can be used to move the cursor from one column in the box to another (<Shift+Tab> moves the cursor backwards), or alternatively you can move directly to a desired field by holding the <Alt> key down and pressing the underlined letter in the field name. Within a column of options you must use the arrow keys to move from one to another. Having selected an option or typed in information, you must press a command button such as the **OK** or **Cancel** button, or choose from additional options.

To select the **OK** button with the mouse, simply point and click, while with the keyboard, you must first press the <Tab> key until the dotted rectangle moves to the required button, and then press the <Enter> key. Pressing <Enter> at any time while a dialogue box is open, will cause the marked items to be selected and the box to be closed.

Some dialogue boxes contain List boxes which show a column of available choices. If there are more choices than can be seen in the area provided, use the scroll bars to reveal them. To select a single item from a List box, either

17

double-click the item, or use the arrow keys to highlight the item and press <Enter>. Other dialogue boxes contain Option buttons with a list of mutually exclusive items. The default choice is marked with a black dot against its name, while unavailable options are dimmed. Other dialogue boxes contain Check boxes which offer a list of options you can switch on or off. Selected options show a cross in the box against the option name.

To cancel a dialogue box, either press the **Cancel** button, or the <Esc> key. Pressing the <Esc> key in succession, closes one dialogue box at a time, and eventually aborts the menu option.

The Status Bar:
This is located along the bottom of the Ami Pro window and is divided into nine sections, as shown below. These can only be accessed by clicking on them with the mouse pointer.

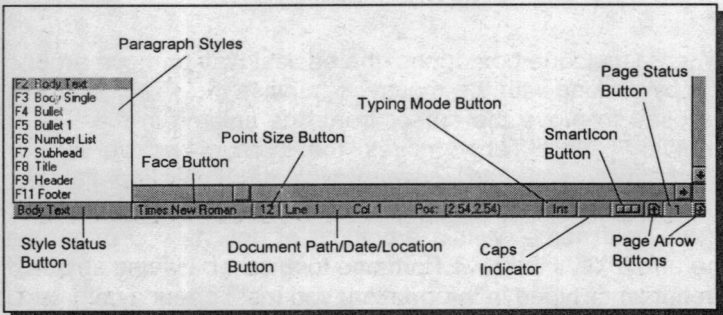

The STYLE STATUS button on the left shows the style of the current paragraph; the one containing the cursor. By clicking this button a list of all the available styles, in the active style sheet, is produced (as shown above). Clicking on one of these will change the style of the current paragraph.

The FACE, or FONT, button shows the current typeface. Clicking on this will enable you to change the typeface of any selected text.

The POINT SIZE button shows the size of selected text. This size can be changed by clicking open the available list and selecting another size.

The DOCUMENT PATH/DATE/LOCATION button changes the information displayed as it is clicked. As shown, it is set to display the line, column and page position of the insertion point (or cursor). The units for page position depend on the settings in the **Modify Page Layout** option of the **Page** menu, as shown below. They can be set to inches, centimetres, picas or points.

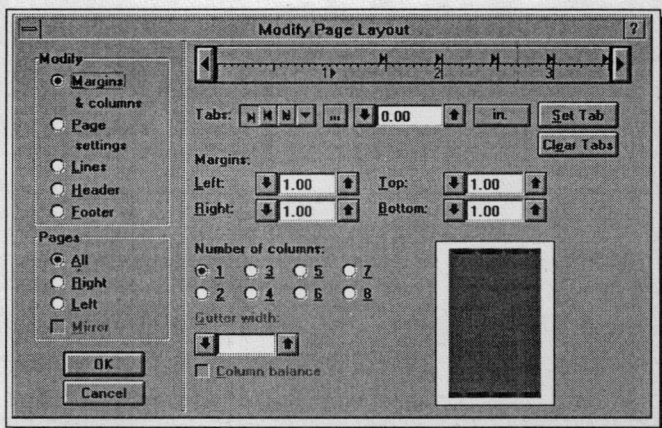

The TYPING MODE button toggles between Insert, Overstrike and Revision marking modes. If your typed text suddenly comes out in blue italic and a vertical line appears in the left margin you have probably inadvertently selected the revision Mode. To change back to normal, switch off this mode by clicking on the Typing Mode button, highlight the offending text, select **Revision marking** from the **Tools** sub-menu and click on the **Accept All Rev** button.

The CAPS button simply displays when the <Caps Lock> key is operational.

The SMARTICONS button is one of the most useful features of the Status Bar. This allows you to control the display of the SmartIcon bar, which is initially at the top of the screen.

Opening this button allows you to select one of the ten sets of SmartIcons provided, or to turn off the SmartIcon bar. The screen display below shows that the Default set is active when Ami Pro is first started.

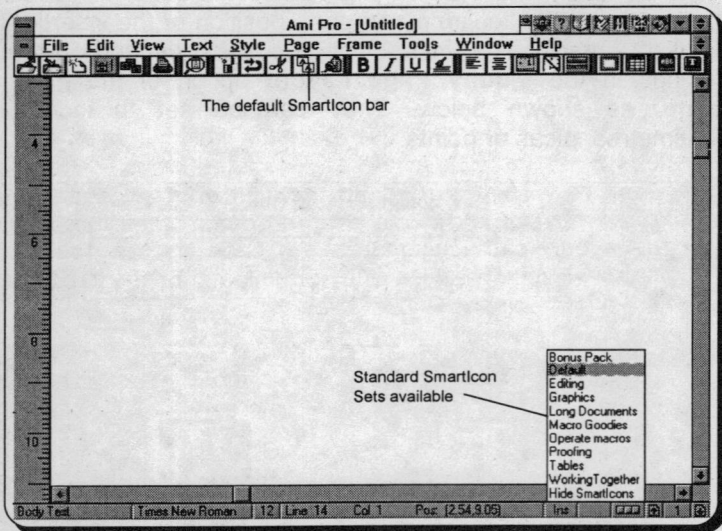

The default SmartIcon bar

Standard SmartIcon
Sets available

Bonus Pack
Default
Editing
Graphics
Long Documents
Macro Goodies
Operate macros
Proofing
Tables
WorkingTogether
Hide SmartIcons

Clicking on either of the two PAGE ARROW buttons moves you to the top of the previous, or next, page respectively. They have the same function as the <Ctrl+PgUp> and <Ctrl+PgDn> keystrokes.

The PAGE STATUS button displays the current document page number. Clicking on this button opens the 'Go To' dialogue box shown. The page number box should be already highlighted so to jump to a distant part of your document you simply type in its page

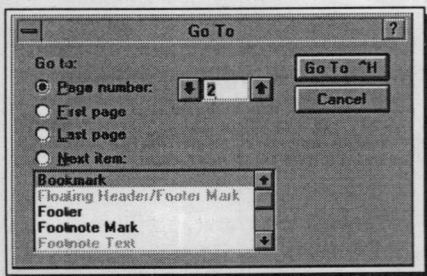

number and press <Enter>. This box also allows quick access to a list of other editing features, as shown.

Your Mouse and Ami Pro
As with all other graphical based programs, the use of a mouse makes many operations both easier and more fun to carry out.

Mouse Pointers:
Ami has 16 different mouse pointers which it uses for its various functions. These are all illustrated below. When the program is initially started up the first you will see is the hourglass, which turns into a large I-beam when the pointer is over your text editing area. As soon as the pointer is moved over the borders, menus or dialogue boxes it changes to an upward pointing hollow arrow.

I	**I-beam**	In normal text areas of screen.
	Arrow	Selecting pointer over menus, bars, boxes, frames, icon bars, etc.
	Copy arrow	When drag-copying text.
	Move arrow	When drag-moving text.
	**Hourglass**	Waiting while Ami Pro is perorming a function.
	**Frame arrow**	While manually creating a frame.
	Fast Format text	When carrying out fast formatting with text format only.
	Fast Format par.	When carrying out fast formatting with paragraph format.

 ?	**Question mark**	When <Shift+F1> is used, you can point and click this pointer on any screen item to get instant Help on it.
☝	**Help hand**	In help windows, used to access 'hypertext' type links.
✋	**Frame hand**	When the inside of a picture frame is double clicked, to move the picture within the frame.
✜	**4-Headed arrow**	In a table over a grid line, used to alter the size of cells.
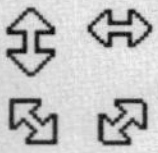 ↕ ↔ ⤡ ⤢	**Double arrows**	Over the border of a window, or the side of a frame, used to drag the side and alter the size of the window, or frame.

Mouse Shortcuts:

While on the subject of your mouse there are several mouse shortcuts in Ami which will save you a lot of time and hassle.

Result	*Mouse action required*
Copy text	Select text, release the mouse button, hold <Ctrl> and drag pointer.
Move text	Select text, release the mouse button and drag pointer to destination.
Select word	Double-click in the word.
Select sentence	Hold <Ctrl> and click in sentence.

Select paragraph	Hold <Ctrl> and double-click in the paragraph.
Select multiple words	Double-click and drag.
Select mult. sentences	Hold <Ctrl>, click and drag.
Select mult. paragraphs	Hold <Ctrl>, double-click and drag.
Modify page layout	Click the right mouse button with the pointer in the margin area.
Modify frame layout	Select frame by left clicking in it and click the right mouse button.
Modify style	Click the right mouse button while the pointer is in the main document area.

Until you get familiar with these actions take care, as the selecting action can sometimes be a little jerky. If the result is not as you expected you can always use the **Edit**, **Undo** command (<Ctrl+Z>) to return to where you started.

Using Help in Ami Pro
Using the Microsoft Windows Help Program, Ami Pro provides on-line Help for every function. You can re-size, move, tile, or cascade the Help window and the current document so that you can keep both of them displayed and you can even copy and edit text from the Help windows into a document. Some of this page was created in this way!

There are several ways to obtain on-line Help:

On-line Help Messages:
Ami Pro displays a command description in the title bar when you choose a menu or command.

Context Sensitive Help:
Simply press **F1** to get instant help on any menu function that you are carrying out. If you are not using a menu box you will

bring up the Help Contents window. The <Esc> key will close a Help window and return you to your original screen.

Point and Shoot Help:

Press <Shift+F1> to obtain a question mark pointer, you can point and click this pointer on any screen item to get instant help on it.

Help Menu:

Choose **Help**, to display the shown menu. Choose **Contents** to display Ami Pro Contents, (or choose another Help menu item to display that Help topic, such as **How Do I?**) and select the Help topic you want. With the keyboard, press <Tab> to select the desired topic and then press <Enter>.

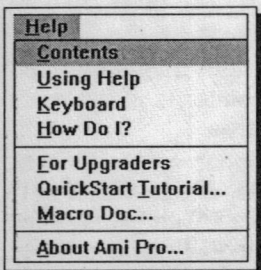

Spend some time exploring the Help system. Most of the Ami Pro manual contents are in it; you just have to find them. A quick way to start would be to select **Using Help**, read each screen of information and then click the **>>** button to move to the next page. Many Help topics contain cross-references to other related Help topics, which display in green. These are often known as 'hypertext, links, and clicking the hand mouse pointer on them displays their content.

Help
Contents
Using Help
Keyboard
How Do I?
For Upgraders
QuickStart Tutorial...
Macro Doc...
About Ami Pro...

3. THE WINDOWS ENVIRONMENT

Manipulating Windows

Ami Pro, which works under Microsoft Windows, allows the display of multiple windows. At some stage you may need to manipulate a series of windows, by selecting which one is to be active, by moving them so that you can see all the relevant parts, or indeed by re-sizing them. What follows is a short discussion on how to manipulate windows.

Changing the Active Window:

To select the active window amongst those displayed on the screen, point to it and click the left mouse button, or, if you are in full screen mode, choose the **Window** option of the main menu and select the appropriate number of the window you want to make the active one.

Moving Windows and Dialogue Boxes:

When you have multiple windows or dialogue boxes on the screen, you might want to move a particular one to a different part of the screen. This can be achieved with either the mouse or the keyboard, but not if the window occupies the full screen, for obvious reasons.

To move a window, or a dialogue box, with the mouse, point to the title bar and drag it (press the left button and keep it pressed while moving the mouse) until the shadow border is where you want it to be. Then release the mouse button to fix it into its new position.

To move with the keyboard, press **Alt+<Spacebar>** to reveal the Application Control menu, or **Alt+<->** to reveal the Document Control menu. Then, press **m** to select **Move** which causes a four-headed arrow to appear in the title bar and use the arrow keys to move the shadow border of the window to the required place. Press <Enter> to fix the window to its new position or <Esc> to cancel the relocation.

Sizing a Window:

You can change the size of a window with either the mouse or the keyboard. To size an active window with the mouse, move the window so that the side you want to change is visible, then move the mouse pointer to the edge of the window or corner so that it changes to a two-headed arrow, then drag the two-headed arrow in the direction you want that side or corner to move. Continue dragging until the shadow border is the size you require, then release the mouse button.

To size with the keyboard, press either **Alt+<Spacebar>** or **Alt+<->** to reveal the Application Control menu or the Document Control menu, then press **s** to select <u>S</u>ize which causes the four-headed arrow to appear. Now press the arrow key that corresponds to the edge you want to move, or if a corner, press the two arrow keys (one after the other) corresponding to the particular corner, which causes the pointer to change to a two-headed arrow. Press an appropriate arrow key in the direction you want that side or corner to move and continue to do so until the shadow border is the size you require, then press <Enter> to fix the new window size.

Minimising and Maximising Windows:

Ami Pro can be minimised into an icon at the bottom of the screen; you may want to do this if you have another Windows application running and need to change over to it. This can be done by either using the mouse to click at the 'Minimise' button (the downward arrow in the upper-right corner of the window), or by pressing **Alt+<Spacebar>** or **Alt+<->** to reveal the Application Control menu or the Document Control menu, and selecting **n** for **Mi<u>n</u>imise**.

To maximise a window so that it fills the entire screen, either click on the 'maximise' button (the upward arrow in the upper-right corner of the window), or press **Alt+<Spacebar>** or **Alt+<->** to display the Application Control menu or the Document Control menu, and select **x** for **Ma<u>x</u>imise**.

An application which has been minimised or maximised can be returned to its original size and position on the screen by either double clicking on its icon to expand it to a window, or clicking on the double-headed button in the upper-right corner of the maximised window to reduce it to its former size. With the keyboard, press **Alt+<Spacebar>** to display the Application Control menu, or **Alt+<->** to display the Document Control menu, and select **r** for **<u>R</u>estore**.

Closing a Window

Ami Pro itself, or a document window, can be closed at any time to save screen space and memory. To close a window either double click on the Control menu button (the large hyphen in the upper-left corner of the window, or press **Alt+<->** and select **c** for **Close** from the Control menu.

If you have made any changes to a document since the last time you saved it, Ami Pro will warn you with the appearance of a dialogue box asking confirmation prior to closing it.

Windows Display Arrangement

The default layout of multiple windows on display on your computer's screen is in 'cascade' form - that is, overlapping one another, with each newly opened window being located slightly below and to the right of the previous one.

The menu option **Window** allows you the choice of having multiple windows automatically displayed in either 'cascade' or 'tile' form. Which way you choose to display multiple windows is a matter of balance between personal preference and the type of work you are doing at the time. Below, we show the cascade type of display arrangement.

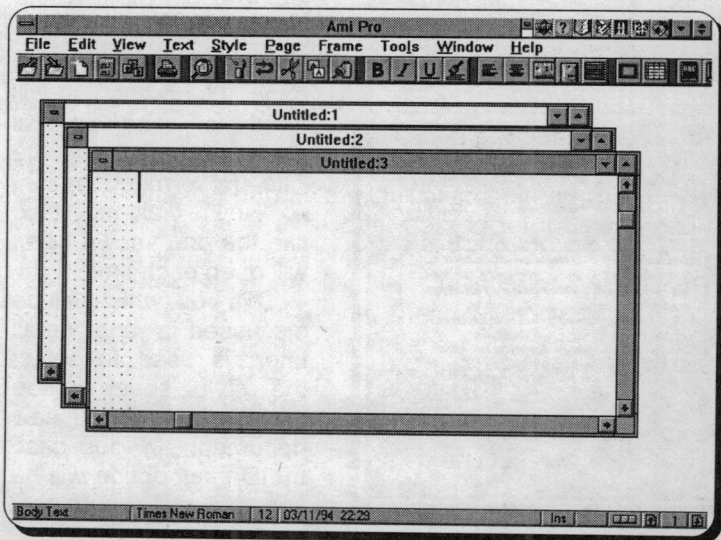

The same document windows will arrange themselves automatically in the display form shown below, when the 'Tile' option is selected.

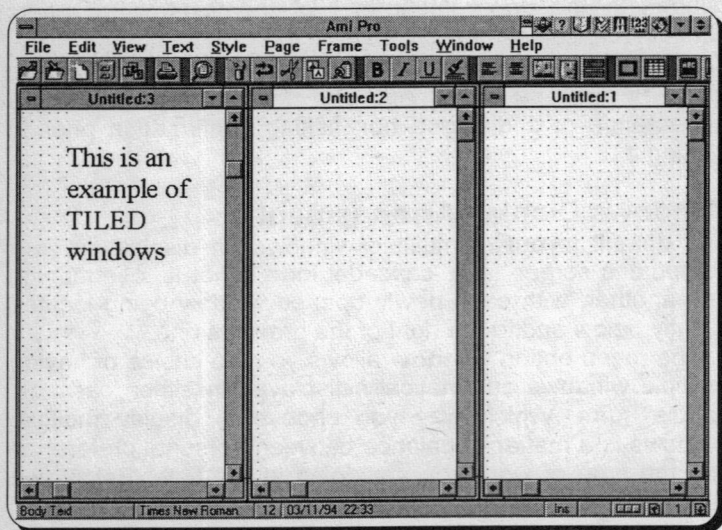

Try arranging the various windows as shown on the next page. To do this you will need to open several documents by using the **File**, **New** menu option. A 'New' dialogue box, like the one shown here, will open each time.

This box, which will be discussed in more detail later, is used to select the style sheet to be used by the new document. In our case the Default option will be fine, but make sure that the **Close Current File** box is not selected. This will ensure that when new files are opened the existing ones will not be automatically closed.

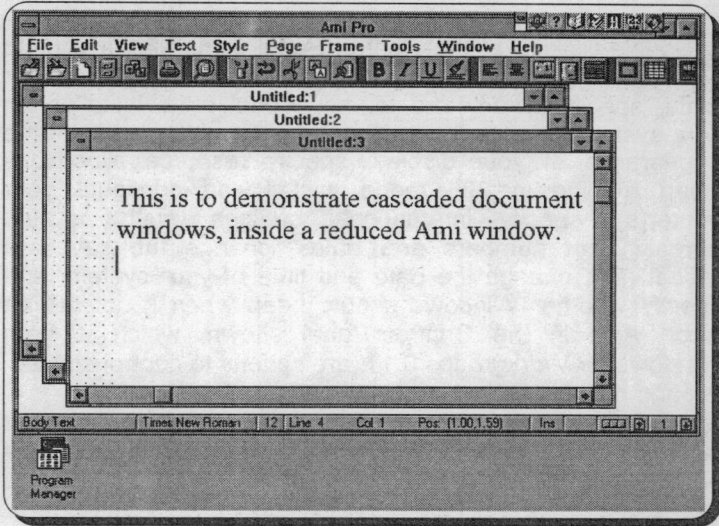

The Windows Control Panel

The Control Panel provides a quick and easy way to change the hardware and software settings of your system. For the sake of completeness we describe its use at this point.

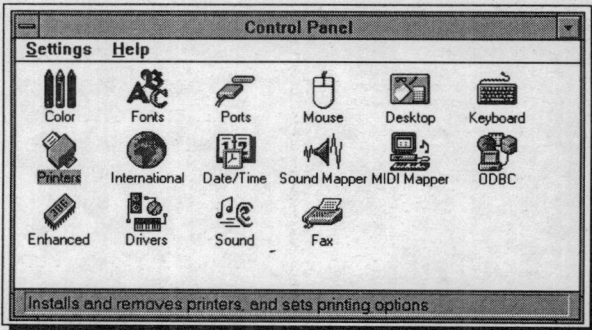

Access to the Control Panel, from within Ami Pro, is from the Application Control Menu box, situated at the left end of the Title Bar. Selecting the **Control Panel** option opens the above window from which the various Control Panel options can be accessed.

Double-clicking at the Control Panel icons allows you to change the display colours, change the display and printer fonts, specify parameters for any serial ports installed on your system, change the settings of your mouse, change the appearance of your display, specify resource allocations when running in 386 mode, install and configure your printer(s), specify international settings, such as the formatting of numbers and dates, change the keyboard repeat rate, change the date and time of your system, and specify whether Windows should beep when it detects an error. Also in the Control Panel shown, which is from Windows for Workgroups 3.11, are options to control sounds, fax and multimedia type operations.

All of the features in your control panel set the environment in which the Ami Pro package operates and you should become familiar with them.

4. AMI PRO DOCUMENT BASICS

In Chapter 2 we spent some time looking at the initial Ami Pro screen, shown on page 11. When the program is first used all the features default to those shown. It is quite possible to use Ami in this mode, without changing any main settings, but as we work through the next two chapters we will explore some of the package's very powerful features, which will allow you to do much more than just the basics.

Entering Text:

Before going any further start Ami Pro, if necessary, and type the memo displayed below into a new document. The text may not be relevant to you, but it will give us a chance to illustrate some of Ami's capabilities.

As you type in text, any time you want to force a new line, or paragraph, just press <Enter>. While typing within a paragraph, Ami Pro sorts out line lengths automatically, without you having to press any keys to move to a new line. This is known as 'word wrap'. If you make a mistake while typing, press the <BkSp> key enough times to erase the mistake and type the text again.

If you want to type text indented from the left margin (like the last entry of the text below), use the <Tab> key before typing the information. Ami Pro has tab stops at every half inch by default. Formatting with tabs will be discussed later.

MEMO TO PC USERS

Personal Computers
The microcomputers in the DP room are a mixture of IBM PS/2s (with 3.5" drives of 1.44MB capacity), IBM ATs (with 5.25" high density drives of 1.2MB capacity) and some IBM compatible machines, which are connected to various printers. As these only have 5.25" drives of 360kB capacity, before printing a document it must be saved on a 360kB format disc.

The computer you are using will have at least a 40MB hard disc on which a number of software programs have been installed. To make life easier, the hard disc is highly structured with each program installed in a separate directory. On switching the computer on, the following prompt is displayed:

    C:\>

Style Sheets:

As you type you should notice that the Style Status button, in the bottom left of the screen, contains the words **Body Text**. This means that all the text you have entered is at the moment shown in the Body Text style. As mentioned previously, every document produced by Ami Pro has to use a Style Sheet. By default the style sheet '_default.sty' is used and at this stage we will not change this. The style sheet contains, both the document page settings and a set of formatting instructions which can be rapidly applied to paragraphs within a document.

To demonstrate this, let's reformat our rather boring looking memo. Click your left mouse button in the title line to place the cursor there, open the Style Status button (by left clicking on it) and select the line **F8 Title**. Your title line should have been instantly reformatted. The **F8** in the above line means that you could also have pressed that key instead of using the Style button. In fact the title line has been converted to centred and bold text, with Arial typeface of point size 18.

You can check that this is true by right clicking your mouse with the cursor still placed in the title line. This will open up the Modify Style dialogue box below:

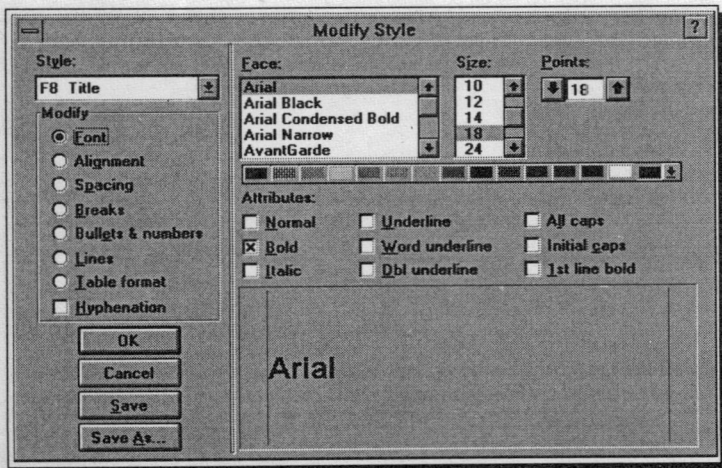

This box is used to control and change styles; glance at it now, but we will come back to it later. The boxes at the top show that the Title style is current and that the **Face** and **Size** are Arial, 18 points; note also that the **Bold** Attribute box is checked.

The window at the bottom shows an example of text with the current format selections. This is a feature of Ami Pro which allows previews wherever they are needed. We are sure that you will experiment a little in this box, but be sure not to save your selections and when you exit do so with the **Cancel** button.

Now return to the memo and select the following styles. With the cursor in the second line of text select **F7 Subhead**, select the first paragraph of text, click on **F5 Bullet 1** and to do it a different way, place the cursor in the second large paragraph of text and press **F5**. Your memo should look quite presentable now, as shown below:

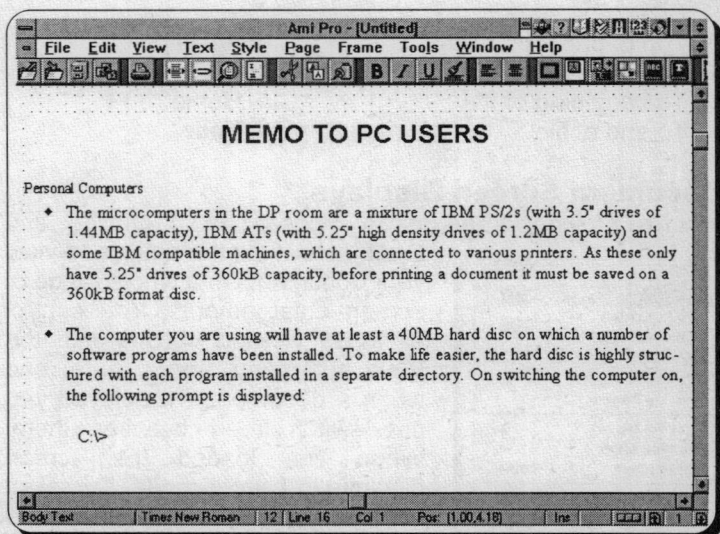

Moving Around a Document:

You can move the cursor around a document with the normal direction keys, with the key combinations shown overleaf, or in a multi-page document, with the **Go To** command (or press <Ctrl+H>), which allows you to jump to a specified page number.

To move	*Press*
Left one character	←
Right one character	→
Up one line	↑
Down one line	↓
Left one word	Ctrl+←
Right one word	Ctrl+→
Beginning of line	Home
End of line	End
Previous sentence	Ctrl+, (comma)
Next sentence	Ctrl+. (full stop)
Paragraph beginning	Ctrl+↑
Paragraph end	Ctrl+↓
Up one screen	PgUp
Down one screen	PgDn
Top of previous page	Ctrl+PgUp
Top of next page	Ctrl+PgDn
To beginning of file	Ctrl+Home
To end of file	Ctrl+End

Document Screen Displays

Ami Pro provides three display modes, Layout, Outline and Draft, as well as the options to view your documents in a whole range of screen enlargements. You control all these viewing options with the **View** sub-menu, shown here, and when a document is displayed you can switch freely between them. When first loaded the screen displays in Layout mode. To select another mode as a default, choose **Tools**, **User Setup**, followed by **Load**, and then select the desired mode.

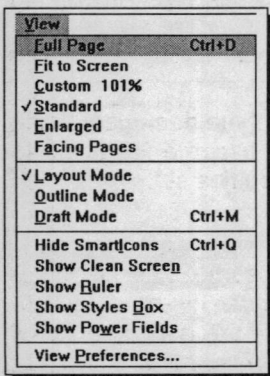

View menu:

```
View
Full Page              Ctrl+D
Fit to Screen
Custom 101%
√ Standard
Enlarged
Facing Pages

√ Layout Mode
Outline Mode
Draft Mode             Ctrl+M

Hide SmartIcons        Ctrl+Q
Show Clean Screen
Show Ruler
Show Styles Box
Show Power Fields

View Preferences...
```

Layout mode:

Layout mode provides a WYSIWYG (what you see is what you get) view of a document. The text displays in the typefaces and point sizes you specify, and with the attributes specified, (alignment, indention, spacing, etc.).

All frames, tables, graphics, headers, footers, and footnotes appear on the screen as they will in the final printed document.

Draft mode:

Draft mode provides a less formatted view of a document. Text displays with attributes and enhancements, but without page breaks, headers, footers, or footnotes. Tables and text, or graphics, in anchored frames display in the correct locations, but other types of frames do not appear on the screen at all. You can edit the contents of a frame in Draft mode, but you cannot manipulate the frame itself.

Outline mode:

Outline mode provides a collapsible view of a document, which enables you to see its organisation at a glance. You can display all the text in a file, or just the text that uses the paragraph styles you specify. Using Outline mode, you can quickly rearrange large sections of text. Some people like to create an outline of their document first, consisting of all the headings, then to sort out the document structure and finally fill in the text. Outline mode is ideal for this type of working method.

Different Document Views

Ami Pro allows five main screen views of the document being worked on, plus an extra one if you use the **View fit to screen** macro provided in the Macro Goodies set.

Standard View:

This shows the screen page in the same size as other Microsoft Windows applications. In Standard view, if you are using a small font, you may need to use the horizontal scroll bar to view both the beginning and end of your lines.

Custom View:

This view is fully editable and allows you to specify how much of the page will display. You control this view by selecting **View**, **View Preferences** and setting the **Custom view** level in the dialogue box as shown below.

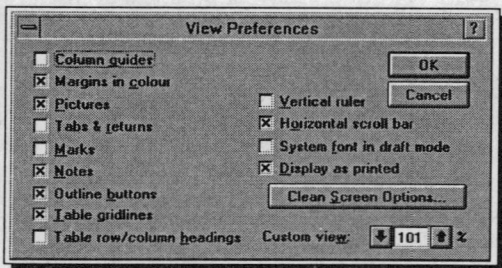

You can specify a percentage size between 10 and 400, where 100% represents the same as Standard view.

Fit to Sceen View:

When you have run the macro **fit2scrn.smm** and select this option the program calculates the Custom view percentage necessary to just fit your page margins on the screen and then selects it for you. You may find this view most useful.

Full Page View:

This view 'shrinks your document' so that you can see an entire page on the screen. It is only available when you are in Layout mode, but is still fully editable. With it you may not be able to read all your document's text, but it can be very useful for checking on the layout of your pages, or for getting a rough overview of the document.

Enlarged View:

Enlarged view doubles the size of Standard view and allows you to zoom quickly to a portion of a page so that you can see fine details of your layout. This view is also fully editable and is most useful when using very small fonts.

Facing Pages View:

You cannot edit your document in the Facing Pages view, it is only available in Layout mode and displays two facing pages side by side. If the cursor is on page one of a document when you choose this view, Ami Pro displays pages one and two next to each other on the screen. If the insertion point is on any other page, Ami Pro displays the even-numbered page on the left of the screen and the odd numbered page on the right; this is the usual way a book is numbered. To return to the previous view level select **Cancel** or press <Esc >.

Using Clean Screen:

You can use the **Show Clean Screen** option to display certain parts of the Ami Pro window and hide other parts. You can do this in all three modes and all views. If you operate Clean Screen in its default mode, with only the **Return Icon** box checked as shown, you can make the screen look like a blank piece of paper.

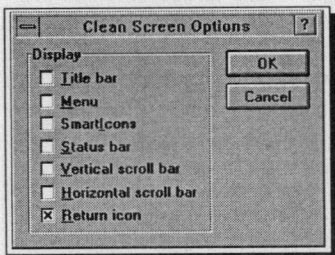

You can select the parts of the Ami Pro window you want to display by clicking in the relevant box, either before or after you choose Clean Screen. You can also specify whether you want to use Clean Screen as a program default by making a selection in the **Tools**, **User Setup**, **Load** command to display the 'Load Defaults' box shown here. While in Clean Screen 'mode' you can access any menu by pressing **Alt+** the under-lined letter of the desired menu. To display the usual Ami

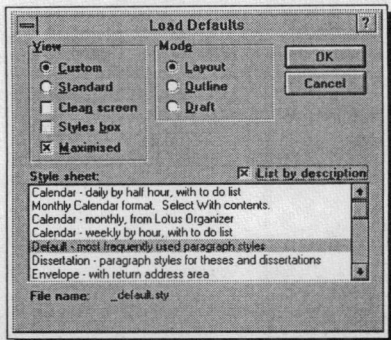

37

Pro window press **Alt+V** to display the **View** Menu and choose **Hide Clean Scree**n; or if you selected **Return icon** in the 'Clean Screen Options' dialogue box, you can click this to display the full Ami Pro window.

If you operate much with a Clear Screen you will need to learn the keyboard shortcuts for commands which are listed in Appendix A. These give you access to most of the more common menu commands without having to open the menu bars.

We leave it to you now to have fun exploring the different modes and views available in Ami Pro.

Changing Default Options

While the above 'Load Defaults' box is on the page perhaps we should say a little more about it. You make selections here to control the Mode, View and Style sheet that will load whenever you start up the program. The **View**, **Styles box** option allows you to display a style window at the top of the screen, similar to that in the original versions of Ami. The **Maximized** option, if selected, will ensure that Ami Pro uses a full screen window to start up in. The other options allow you to select view and mode defaults.

User Setup:

When you have finished with the 'Load Default' box you will be returned to the 'User Setup' box which should be similar to that shown here. This is in fact the first of several set-up boxes. It allows you to customise the program to start and run as you wish. In the File Saving section you can set Ami Pro to create automatic backups of files, in another directory, when they are saved; and to automatically save

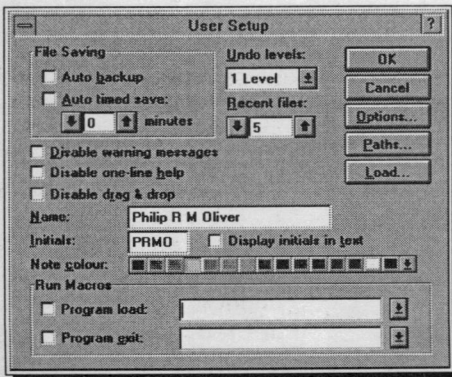

the current file at regular intervals. The last can be a dangerous option if you are working on a detailed document, change your mind and need to return to its original, only to find it has been replaced.

We find it far safer to manually save our work at regular intervals using the keyboard accelerator combination <Ctrl+S>.

The **Undo levels** option gives you a choice of 1 to 4 back editing levels. The level you choose determines the number of actions or levels Ami Pro will reverse, or undo. You can also turn this option off. One thing to remember is that the fewer the levels of Undo, the faster Ami Pro will operate.

You can also specify the number of recent file names you want to display at the end of the **File** menu. Ami Pro will display the names of up to 5 of the most recently opened files, you can then opt to open any of these by simply clicking the sub-menu.

You can disable the following Ami Pro procedures by checking the relevant box.

Disable warning messages stops the display of messages warning you that you are about to delete certain format marks from your document.

Disable one-line help prevents the display of command help descriptions in the title bar.

Disable drag & drop for moving or copying text with the mouse pointer. Select this if you do editing that does not require moving or copying text.

There are options to control the colour of inserted notes and to specify whether your initials are to be placed in a document during editing operations. This facility is really only useful when several people need to check a document.

Finally you can specify a macro you want to run automatically either when you start, or exit from, Ami Pro.

The **Options** button opens a box which controls advanced typographical options, such as hyphenation and kerning; and the **Paths** button allows you to change the default paths to your Ami Pro subdirectories.

Saving to a File:

To save a document, use either the **File, Save** or **File, Save As** commands. **Save As** is used when you want to save your document with a different name. A dialogue box appears on the screen, as shown below, with the cursor in the **File name** field box waiting for you to type a name.

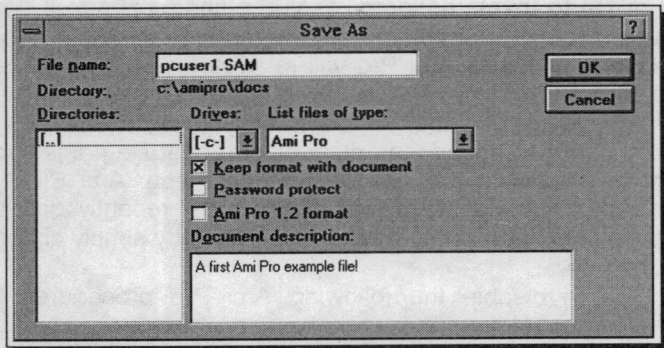

You can select a drive other than the one displayed by clicking the down arrow against the **Drives** field. To save your work type PCUSERS1 into the **File name** box and press **OK**. The program adds the extension .SAM, automatically.

By using the **List files of type** button we could have saved in ASCII, Rich Text Format or another format suitable for other word processing programs.

A useful feature in Ami Pro is the facility to add a **Document description** to every file. To do this you simply place the pointer in the bottom box and type a suitable description, to help you select your file at some stage in the future. As you can see there is a description shown in the example above.

Closing a Document:

There are several ways to close a document in Ami Pro. Once you have saved it you can double click on the Document Control button at the left end of the menu bar; you would usually use this method when you have several files open together.

If you want to open a new, or another, document you can check the **Close current file** box in either the **New** or the **Open** boxes of the **File** menu, as shown on pages 28 and 17 respectively. The current document is then replaced by the new one.

If your document has changed since the last time it was saved you will be given the option to save it, before all is lost.

5. EDITING YOUR DOCUMENTS

Document Editing

It will not be long, when using Ami Pro, before you will need to edit your document. This could include deleting unwanted words, correcting a mistake or adding extra text in the document. All these operations are very easy to carry out.

For small deletions, such as letters or words, the easiest method to adopt is the use of the <Del> or <BkSp> keys. With the <Del> key, position the cursor on the first letter you want to delete and press <Del>; the letter is deleted and the following text moves one space to the left. With the <BkSp> key, position the cursor immediately to the right of the character to be deleted and press <BkSp>; the cursor moves one space to the left pulling the rest of the line with it and overwriting the character to be deleted. Note that the difference between the two is that with <Del> the cursor does not move at all.

Word processing is usually carried out in the insert mode, selected by clicking the Typing mode button on the Status Bar. Any characters typed will be inserted at the cursor location and the following text will be pushed to the right, and down, to make room. To insert blank lines in your text, place the cursor at the beginning of the line where the blank is needed and press <Enter>. To remove the blank line, position the cursor at its leftmost end and press <Del>.

When larger scale editing is needed you have several alternatives with Ami Pro. You can use the **Cut, Copy** and **Paste** operations, after first 'selecting' the text to be altered. These functions are then available when the **Edit** sub-menu is activated. Instead of using the sub-menu you can click on SmartIcon alternatives for all the editing commands. This makes working with a mouse very much easier and quicker. A method, new to Version 3.0 of Ami Pro is to use the 'drag' facility for copying or moving text.

Selecting Text:

The procedure in Ami Pro, as with most Windows based applications, is first to select the text to be altered before any operation, such as formatting or editing, can be carried out on it. Selected text is highlighted on the screen. This can be carried out in two main ways:

a. Using the keyboard; position the cursor on the first character to be selected and hold down the <Shift> key while using the direction keys to highlight the required text, then release the <Shift> key. Navigational key combinations can be used with the <Shift> key to highlight blocks of text. For example, to highlight the text from the present cursor position to the end of the line, use <Shift+End>, while to highlight the text from the present cursor position to the end of the document, use <Shift+Ctrl+End>.

b. With the mouse; press down the left mouse button at the beginning of the block and while holding it pressed, drag the cursor across the block so that the desired text is highlighted, then release the mouse button. To select a word, double-click at the word, to select a sentence, hold the <Ctrl> key down and click in the sentence, or to select a larger block, place the cursor at the beginning of the block, press the <Shift> key down and while holding it pressed, move the mouse pointer to the end of the desired block, and click the left mouse button. The other mouse navigation shortcuts detailed on page 22 can also be used for selecting your text.

Try out both these methods and find out the one you are most comfortable with.

Copying Blocks of Text:

Once text has been selected it can be copied to another location in your present document, to another Ami Pro document, or even to another Windows application, via the clipboard. As with most of the editing and formatting operations there are several ways of doing this.

The first is by using the **Edit, Copy** command sequence from the menu, to copy the selected text to the Windows clipboard, moving the cursor to the start of where you want the copied text to be placed, and using the **Edit, Paste** command.

Another method uses the quick key combinations - <Ctrl+Ins> (or <Ctrl+C>) to copy and <Shift+Ins> (or <Ctrl+V>) to paste - once the text to be copied has been selected, which does not require the menu bar to be activated. As you get used to the Ami Pro package you will be able to save a lot of time by using quick key combinations.

A third method uses the 'Copy to clipboard' and 'Paste clipboard contents' SmartIcons; you can of course only use this method with a mouse (see Appendix B for a detailed list of the SmartIcons available in Ami Pro).

To copy the same text again to another location in the document, move the cursor to the new location and paste it there with any of these methods, as it is stored on the clipboard until it is replaced by the next Cut, or Copy, operation.

The last method for copying text is to 'drag' selected text by holding the <Ctrl> key depressed, clicking and holding down the left mouse button and moving the pointer out of the selected text. The pointer will change to the "copy scissors" and a small red vertical bar will follow the pointer around the screen. Place this bar at the start of where you want the copied text to be and release the mouse button. The new text will insert itself where placed, even if the overstrike mode is in operation. Text copied by dragging is not placed on the clipboard, so multiple copies are not possible, as with the other methods.

Moving Blocks of Text:

Selected text can be moved to any location in the same document. Use the **Edit, Cut,** command or <Shift+Del> (or <Ctrl+X>), or the 'Cut to clipboard' SmartIcon, move the cursor to the required new location and use the same **Paste** actions as described above. The moved text will be placed at the cursor location and will force any existing text to make room for it. This operation can be cancelled by simply pressing <Esc>. Once moved multiple copies of the same text can be produced by other **Paste** operations.

Selected text can be moved by dragging the mouse with the left button held down. The drag pointer is a pair of scissors. As with drag copied text the clipboard is not used.

Deleting Blocks of Text:

When text is cut, it is removed from the document, but placed on the clipboard until further text is either copied or deleted. With Ami Pro any selected text can be deleted by pressing **Edit, Cut,** or by pressing the <Del>, or <BkSp> keys. However, using **Edit, Cut**, allows you to use the **Edit, Paste** command, but using the <Del> or <BkSp> key does not.

The Undo Command:

As text is lost with the delete command you should use it with caution, but if you do make a mistake all is not lost as long as you act promptly. The **Edit, Undo** command reverses your most recent editing or formatting commands if the Undo Level in User Setup is set to one or more levels. You need to use it before carrying out any further operations however. Undo does not reverse any action once editing changes have been saved to file. Only editing done after the save can be reversed. Ami Pro can be set to Undo changes made up to 4 levels deep, but unless you have a jet propelled computer you will find this setting slows the program down too much. One level back should be enough for most people!

Finding and Changing Text:

Ami Pro allows you to search for specifically selected text, or character combinations, using the **Edit**, **Find & Replace** command. This opens a dialogue box as shown. In the **Find** mode it will highlight each occurrence in turn so that you can carry out some action on it, such as change its font or appearance. In the **Replace all** mode you specify what replacement is to be automatically carried out. For example, in a long article you may decide, as above, to replace every occurrence of the word 'oranges' with the words 'apples and oranges'.

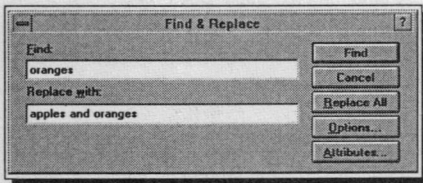

The Options box lets you control how the search is carried out. You can force both the search and the replace operations to work with whole words only, exact text case or

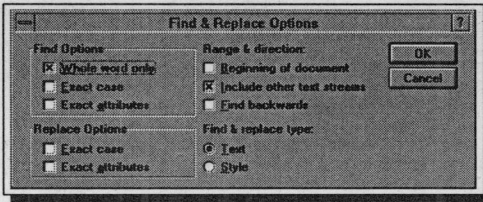

Find & Replace Options

Find Options
- [X] Whole word only
- [ ] Exact case
- [ ] Exact attributes

Replace Options
- [ ] Exact case
- [ ] Exact attributes

Range & direction:
- [ ] Beginning of document
- [X] Include other text streams
- [ ] Find backwards

Find & replace type:
- (•) Text
- ( ) Style

OK
Cancel

attributes, as listed in the box below. The option **Beginning of document**, as shown above, lets you start the search from the document beginning no matter where the cursor is. Check the **Find backwards** box to do a backward search through your document. The **Include other text streams** allows you to search through text included in frames in the document.

By selecting **Style** you can search for, or replace, different paragraph styles. This can be useful if you develop a new style and want to change all the text of another style in a document to use it.

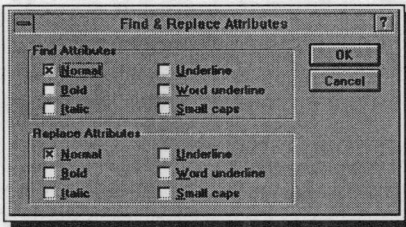

Find & Replace Attributes

Find Attributes
- [X] Normal
- [ ] Bold
- [ ] Italic
- [ ] Underline
- [ ] Word underline
- [ ] Small caps

Replace Attributes
- [X] Normal
- [ ] Bold
- [ ] Italic
- [ ] Underline
- [ ] Word underline
- [ ] Small caps

OK
Cancel

You can search for, and replace, tabs and hard returns, or a combination of both these and text.

The list below gives the key combinations of special characters to type into the **Find** and **Replace with** boxes.

Type	*To find or replace*
Ctrl+Tab	A tab character.
Ctrl+Enter	A hard return.
?	For example, searching for nec? will find such words as necessary, neck, nectar, and connect, to mention but a few, provided they exist in your document and the **Whole word only** option is not selected. If it is selected only 'neck' will be found.

*   Any series of characters in a file. Searching for nec* in the above example would find all the above words regardless of the **Whole word only** option.

Page Breaks:

The program automatically inserts a 'soft' page break in a document when a page of typed text is full. To force a manual, or hard, page break in a document, use the **Page**, **Breaks** menu command and select **Insert page break** in the dialogue box as shown below.

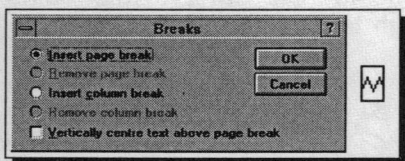

An example of the Ami Pro page break symbol is shown in the right side of the adjacent box. This symbol is only visible if you have selected **Marks** in the **View**, **View Preferences** sub-menu. It attaches itself to the end of the last paragraph of the page on which the mark was placed.

You can delete manual page breaks either from the 'Breaks' dialogue box described, by placing the cursor on the page break mark and pressing the <Del> key, or by deleting selected text which includes a page break. Ami Pro warns you that you are about to delete a page break, as shown here. Press either <Enter> or 'Y' to complete the deletion. The warning is necessary as most of the time you will probably be happy to work without the formatting marks displayed. It is very easy then to accidentally delete pagination in selected text.

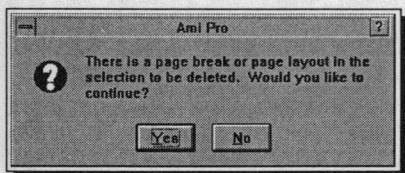

You cannot delete the soft page breaks that the program inserts automatically.

48

Formatting Your Work

Formatting involves the appearance of individual characters or words, the line spacing and alignment of paragraphs, and the overall page layout of the entire document. These functions are carried out in Ami Pro in several different ways. Primary page layout and text formatting is included in the different Style Sheets, which will be discussed in the next chapter. Within any document, however, you can override Paragraph Style formats by applying text formatting and enhancements manually to selected text. If you cancel this manual formatting by selecting the text and pressing <Ctrl+N>, or selecting, **Normal** from the **Text** sub-menu, the format will revert to that in the current paragraph style.

Formatting Text:

The fonts available in Ami Pro depend on the printer(s) you have set-up in Microsoft Windows and selected in Ami with the **File**, **Printer Setup** commands. If the typeface name on the Face button of the Status Bar appears in red it means the font selected is not available to your printer and you should select another one. If you don't, Ami Pro will select the nearest one you do have available and will use that.

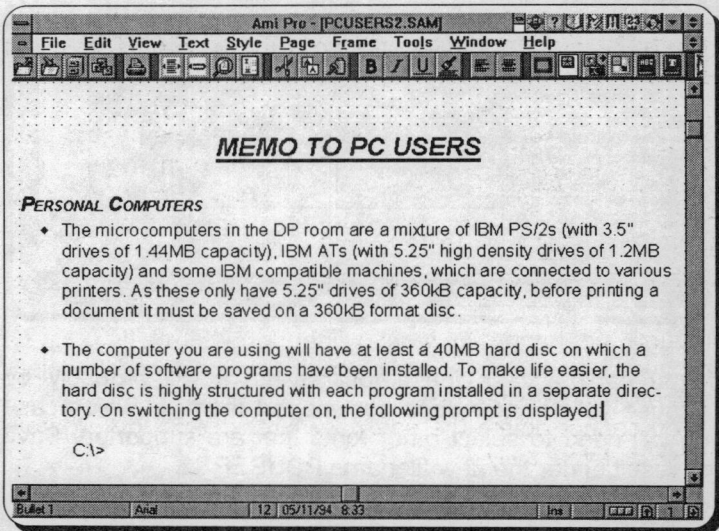

```
┌─────────────────────────────────────────────────────────────┐
│               Ami Pro - [PCUSERS2.SAM]                        │
│  File  Edit  View  Text  Style  Page  Frame  Tools  Window  Help │
│ [toolbar icons]  B I U                                        │
│                                                               │
│                                                               │
│                    MEMO TO PC USERS                           │
│                                                               │
│  PERSONAL COMPUTERS                                            │
│                                                               │
│   ◆ The microcomputers in the DP room are a mixture of IBM PS/2s (with 3.5" │
│     drives of 1.44MB capacity), IBM ATs (with 5.25" high density drives of 1.2MB │
│     capacity) and some IBM compatible machines, which are connected to various │
│     printers. As these only have 5.25" drives of 360kB capacity, before printing a │
│     document it must be saved on a 360kB format disc.         │
│                                                               │
│   ◆ The computer you are using will have at least a 40MB hard disc on which a │
│     number of software programs have been installed. To make life easier, the │
│     hard disc is highly structured with each program installed in a separate direc- │
│     tory. On switching the computer on, the following prompt is displayed│ │
│                                                               │
│       C:\>                                                    │
│                                                               │
│ Bullet 1      Arial        12  05/11/94  8:33        Ins      │
└─────────────────────────────────────────────────────────────┘
```

Originally, the text of the memo PCUSERS1.SAM, which we produced in the last chapter, was typed in the 12 point size Times New Roman typeface of the default style. To change it into what appears on the previous screen dump, first select all the text in the first bullet paragraph, then use the **Text**, **Font** sub-menu, shown here, to format it in Arial 12 point size. Change the title of the memo to underlined, italics, 18 point size Arial and the sub title to italics, small capitals, 14 point size Arial as shown below.

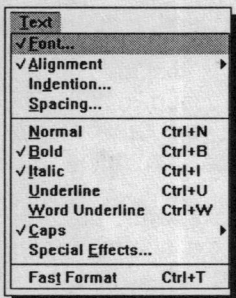

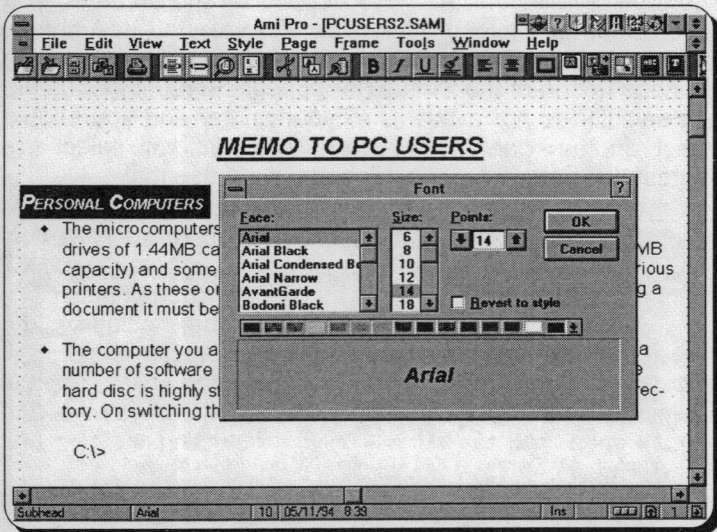

Text	
√ Font...	
√ Alignment	▶
Indention...	
Spacing...	
Normal	Ctrl+N
√ Bold	Ctrl+B
√ Italic	Ctrl+I
Underline	Ctrl+U
Word Underline	Ctrl+W
√ Caps	▶
Special Effects...	
Fast Format	Ctrl+T

Ami Pro - [PCUSERS2.SAM]

File   Edit   View   Text   Style   Page   Frame   Tools   Window   Help

MEMO TO PC USERS

PERSONAL COMPUTERS

♦ The microcomputers   drives of 1.44MB ca   MB
capacity) and some   rious
printers. As these o   g a
document it must be

Font

Face: Size: Points:
Arial   6   ↓ 14 ↑   OK
Arial Black   8   Cancel
Arial Condensed B   10
Arial Narrow   12
AvantGarde   14   □ Revert to style
Bodoni Black   18

Arial

♦ The computer you a   a
number of software   e
hard disc is highly st   ec-
tory. On switching th

C:\>

Subhead   Arial   10 05/11/94 8 39   Ins

If you can't access these font styles, it will probably be because your printer does not support them, in which case you will need to select other fonts that are supported. Save the result under the new filename PCUSERS2.

Some Font Basics:

A 'point' is a unit of measurement, approximately 1/72 of an inch, that determines the height of a character. There is another unit of character measurement called the 'pitch' which is the number of characters that can fit horizontally in one inch. The spacing of a font is either 'fixed' (monospaced) or 'proportional'. With fixed spacing, each character takes up exactly the same space, while proportionally spaced characters take up different spacing (an 'i' or a 't' take up less space than a 'u' or a 'w'). Thus the length of proportionally spaced text can vary depending on which letters it contains. However, numerals take up the same amount of space whether they have been specified as fixed or proportional.

Which fonts you choose is largely dependent on your printer, as mentioned previously. One thing you must bear in mind is that Ami Pro uses screen fonts to display characters on screen and printer fonts to print characters with a printer. If you choose printer fonts for which there are no screen fonts, Ami Pro will use the nearest screen font to display your work, which might not show exactly what you will get when you print your work. It will be the printed document which is in the correct font style.

Windows 3.1 makes available several 'TrueType' fonts which can be used by Windows applications, such as Ami Pro. TrueType fonts are scaleable to any point size and look exactly the same on the screen as they do when printed.

In Ami Pro all manual text formatting, including the selection of typeface, point size, colour, attributes (bold, italic and various underlines), various capitalisation styles, and the special effects of superscript, subscript, overstrike and strikethrough, are carried out by first selecting the text and then doing one of the following:

a. Using the **Text** sub-menu as described above
b. Using keyboard short cuts, when available
c. Using SmartIcons from one of the palettes.

Whichever of the above methods is used the formatting can take place after the text is entered, or the formatting command can be selected before text is entered. Text will then type in the chosen format until a further format command is given. If this method is used, or if Clear Screen view is used the keyboard short cuts will be the fastest method, once you can remember the short cut commands, which are detailed in Appendix A. Normal text (unformatted) can be forced, or selected, with the **Text**, **Normal** sub-menu command (<Ctrl+N>).

While you are entering, or editing, text in the Layout View mode, with some versions of Ami, you may find that when you embolden part of the text the screen display becomes distorted. To solve this, either press <PgDn> followed immediately by <PgUp>, or change to the Draft View mode with the <Ctrl+M> quick key combination.

Text Enhancements

Ami Pro defines a paragraph, as any text which is followed by a paragraph mark, which is created by pressing the <Enter> key. So single line titles, as well as long typed text, can form paragraphs. The paragraph symbol is only visible if you have selected **Marks** in the **View**, **View** **Preferences** sub-menu.

Paragraph Alignment:

Ami Pro allows you to align a paragraph at the left margin (the default), at the right margin, centred between both margins, or justified between both margins. As with most operations there are several ways to perform alignment in Ami Pro, as shown below.

SmartIcon	Text, Alignment Menu	Keystrokes
	Left	<Ctrl+L>
	Centre	<Ctrl+E>
	Right	<Ctrl+R>
	Justify	<Ctrl+J>

Paragraph Spacing:

A paragraph can be displayed on screen or printed on paper in single-line, 1½-line, or double-line spacing, or you can set the spacing to any value you want with the **Custom** option. All alignment and spacing options can easily be selected from the **Text**, **Spacing** sub-menu command. When setting customised line spacing you have the choice of 4 units to work with, inches, cms, points or picas.

Indenting Text:

Most documents with lists, or numbered sections, will require some form of paragraph indenting. An indent is the space between the margin and the edge of the text in the paragraph.

When an indent is set, any justification on that side of the page sets at the indent, not the page border. This can be on the left or right side of the page.

Open the file PCUSERS2, place the cursor in the first paragraph, select the Body Text style from the Style button and action the **Text** menu. The pull-down menu shown on the next page will appear from which you can open the Indention dialogue box by choosing the **Indention** option. In this screen dump both the **Text** sub-menu and the Indention dialogue box are shown together for convenience. On the screen however the menu closes when the box is opened.

File Edit View **Text** Style Page Frame Tools Window Help

√Font...
√Alignment ►
√Indention...
Spacing...

Normal   Ctrl+N
Bold   Ctrl+B
Italic   Ctrl+I
Underline   Ctrl+U
Word Underline Ctrl+W
Caps
Special Effects...

Fast Format   Ctrl+T

C USERS

PERSONAL COMPUT

The microc ... re a mixture of IBM PS/2s (with 3.5"
drives of 1.44 ... h 5.25" high density drives of 1.2MB
capacity) and ... hines, which are connected to various
printers. As th ... of 360kB capacity, before printing a
document it m ... ormat disc.

◆ The compute
number of so
hard disc is h
tory. On switc

C:\>

Indention

Indent
All: ↓ 0.00 ↑   From right: ↓ 0.00 ↑   **OK**
First: ↓ 1.50 ↑   Cancel
Rest: ↓ 1.0 ↑   CM.
☐ Revert to style

Body Text   Arial   12 C:\AMIPRO\DOCS   Ins   1

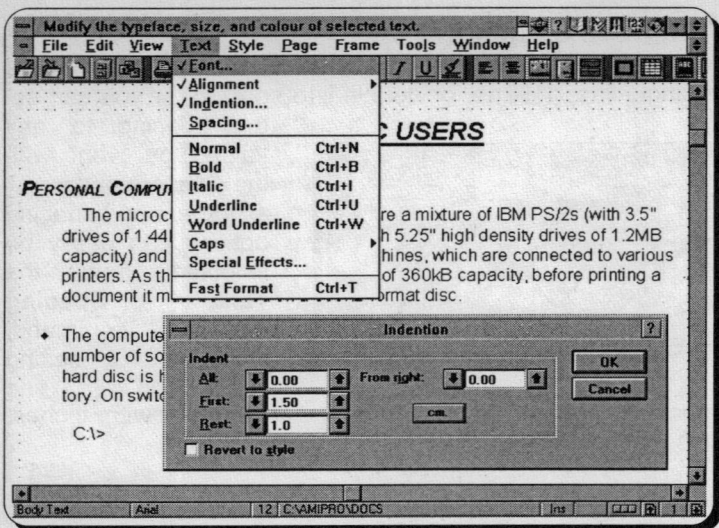

The first paragraph is shown indented which will be the result of typing the values shown in the Indention dialogue box and pressing the **OK** button.

Hanging Indents:

The **Indention** option can be used to create 'hanging' indents, where all the lines in a paragraph, including any text on the first line that follows a tab, are indented by the amount specified in **Rest**. These are often used in lists such as those on page 22. To illustrate the method, use the PCUSERS1 file and add at the end of it, after the 'C:\>' prompt, the text shown in the first screen on the next page. This screen dump, incidentally, was produced from a Clean Screen view, showing the return icon in the bottom right corner and the SmartCenter bar above. After you have typed it in, save the enlarged memo as PCUSERS3, before going on with formatting the new information. This is done as a precaution in case anything goes wrong with the formatting - it is sometimes much easier to reload a saved file (using either the **File, Open**, or the **Revert to Saved** command), than it is to try to unscramble a wrongly formatted document!

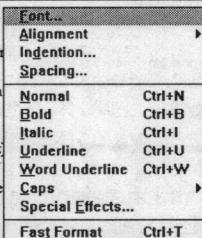

C:\>

To find out what is on your hard disc, type

DIR   (and press the <Enter> key)

which will produce a list of all the directories and filenames on the 'Root' directory (the one with the C:\> prompt) - directories are displayed with their names in angle brackets, for example, <DOS>. If your hard disc is structured correctly, then each program package will be installed in a separate directory. For example:

Name Description

LOTUS Holds the LOTUS 1-2-3 spreadsheet package.

QBASIC Holds the Quick Basic suite of programs which allow you to write fully structured Basic programs and compile them. It is one of the best versions of Basic available.

QA Holds the Q&A package which is an integrated Database and Word Processor.

In general, using a computer effectively involves learning the operating system, in this case MS-DOS, and then learning each package you are going to use.

Now select the text in paragraphs 4 to 7, choose the **Text**, **Indention** command, and type the figures shown in the screen below, into the **First** and **Rest** field boxes of the 'Indention' dialogue box.

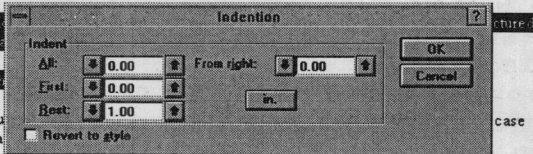

As before both the **T**ext sub-menu and the 'Indention' dialogue box are shown together for convenience in this example, you will not see them together.

After selecting **OK** the text is still highlighted, so click the mouse button on the page, or press <Esc>, to remove the highlight. The second and following lines of the third paragraph selected should have been indented 1 inch from the left margin. This is still not very inspiring, so to complete the effect we will edit the first lines of each paragraph, to end up with the display below:

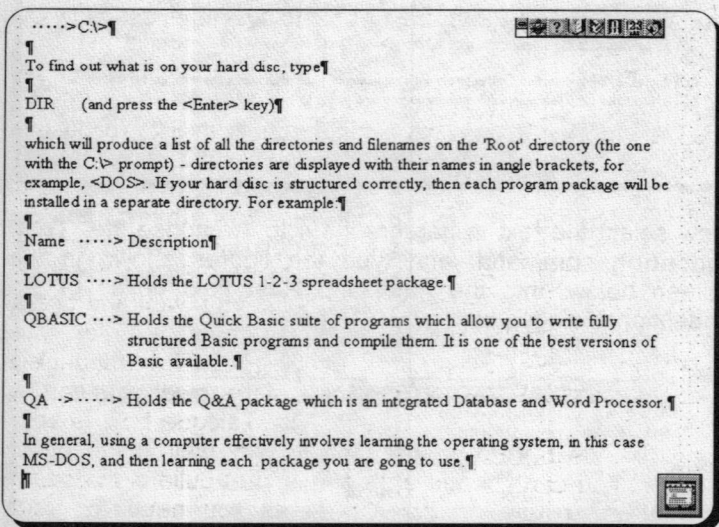

```
·····>C:\>¶
¶
To find out what is on your hard disc, type¶
¶
DIR     (and press the <Enter> key)¶
¶
which will produce a list of all the directories and filenames on the 'Root' directory (the one
with the C:\> prompt) - directories are displayed with their names in angle brackets, for
example, <DOS>. If your hard disc is structured correctly, then each program package will be
installed in a separate directory. For example:¶
¶
Name  ·····> Description¶
¶
LOTUS ·····> Holds the LOTUS 1-2-3 spreadsheet package.¶
¶
QBASIC ···> Holds the Quick Basic suite of programs which allow you to write fully
                structured Basic programs and compile them. It is one of the best versions of
                Basic available.¶
¶
QA  ·> ·····> Holds the Q&A package which is an integrated Database and Word Processor.¶
¶
In general, using a computer effectively involves learning the operating system, in this case
MS-DOS, and then learning each  package you are going to use.¶
¶
```

Place the cursor in front of the word 'Description' in paragraph 4 and press the <Tab> key twice. This places the start of the word in the same column as the indented text above. To complete the effect place Tabs before the word 'Holds' in the next three paragraphs, until your hanging indents are correct.

This may seem like a complicated rigmarole to go through each time you want the hanging indent effect, but with Ami Pro you will eventually set up all your indents, etc., in style sheets. Then all you do is click in a paragraph to produce them. Our 'Book Style' sheet has hanging indent styles for each of the tab positions across the page.

When you finish formatting the document, save it under its current filename with the **File, Save** command (<Ctrl+S>). This command does not display a dialogue box, so you use it when you do not need to make any changes to the saving operation.

Inserting Bullets:

Bullets are small characters you can insert, anywhere you like, in the text of your document to improve the visual display. In Ami Pro there are 17 bullets available, as follows:

. ● ▪ ■ ☐ ◆ ◆ ○ ○ ✓ ► ☐ ☐ ☑ ☒ ➢ ➢

They are normally used to highlight items in lists, or in the middle of a sentence. To place a bullet put the cursor where you want it to appear and select **Edit**, **Insert**, **Bullet**, the following dialogue box will display. Select the type of bullet you want and press **OK** to insert it into your document. The magnified box, at the lower right corner of this dialogue box, is very useful as the bullets do not display very well in the bullet window. You can change the point size of bullets, the same as any other text, to get the effect you need for your document.

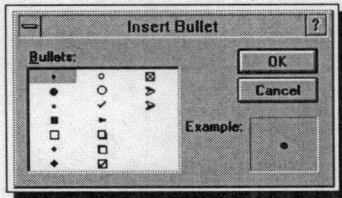

Once inserted you can copy, move or delete a bullet in the same way as any other text.

Inserting Date and Time:

You can insert today's date, the date the current document was created or was last revised, or a date or time that reflects the current system date and time into a document.

Place the insertion point where you want to insert the date, select the **Edit**, **Insert**, **Date/Time** menu commands and fill in the dialogue box produced and shown on the next page.

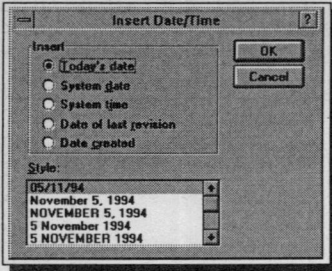

The meanings of the available options are:

Today's date - Permanently inserts the current system date. The document will always display this date, so make sure your system date is correct.

System date/time - Inserts a date/time that is updated to the current system date/time each time you open the document and view that page. This is useful for 'date/time stamping' a printed document. The display of system time is determined by the time format specified in the Windows Control Panel (see page 29).

Date of last revision - Inserts the date you last saved the current document.

Date created - Permanently inserts the date the current document was created.

Inserting a Note:

Another powerful feature of Ami Pro is the facility to place 'notes' anywhere in a document. These act like electronic 'Post It' labels, by default they are even the same yellow colour.

Such notes can be very useful to place reminders in your text. We use them most to mark a stopping position when doing a detailed edit of a document. They can really come into their own if several people view, and edit, the same documents. Every person could then set the default colour of his, or her, notes to a different colour with the **Tools**, **User Setup** options, covered in Chapter 4, and embed notes in the text for the others to read.

You place a note at the cursor position with the **Edit**, **Insert**, **Note** menu commands. A yellow window opens up, with your initials, the note number and the current system date and time on the Title Bar, as shown on the facing page.

Inserting a Note

Another powerful feat... ...e 'notes' anywhere in a ... ...c 'Post It' labels, by de ... ...w colour.

   Such notes can be very useful to place reminders in your text. We use them most to mark a stopping position when doing a detailed edit of a document. They can really come into their own if several people view, and edit, the same documents. Every person could then set the default colour of

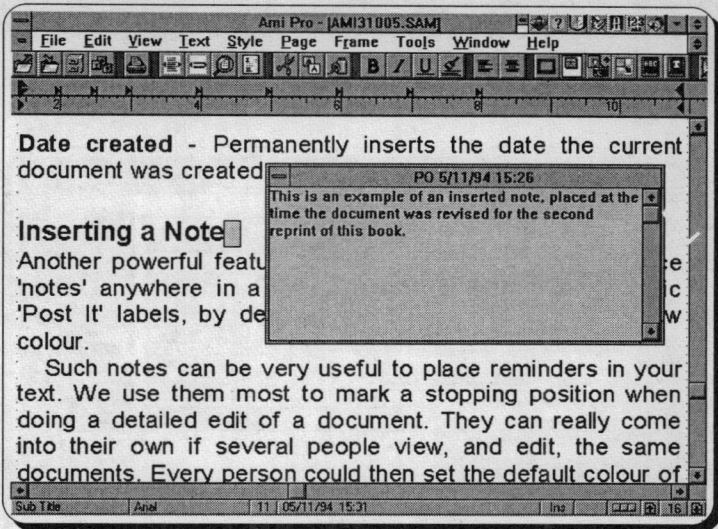

The insertion point is placed in the text area of the note window, ready for you to type in your note. When finished entering text, close the note, either with its command button, or simply by left clicking your mouse outside the window. A small yellow box is left at the note location, which will flow with the text surrounding it. This marker is only visible if you have selected **Notes**, in the **View**, **View Preferences** dialogue box.

   To open a note, when you need to read its contents, double click on it with the mouse pointer. To remove one, either delete it as you would other text, or select **Remove This Note** from the note's command menu.

Printing Documents

When Windows was first installed on your computer the printers you intend to use should have been selected, and the SETUP program should have installed the appropriate printer drivers. Before printing for the first time, you would be wise to ensure that your printer is in fact properly installed.

To do this open the Window's Control Panel, as described at the end of Chapter 3 and double click on the 'Printers' icon. This will open the **Printers** box shown below.

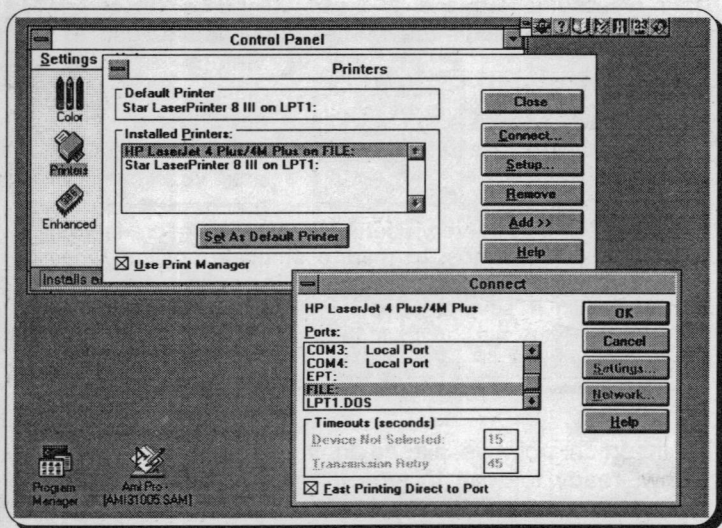

Here, two printer drivers have been installed; a Star LaserPrinter as the 'default' printer, configured for output via the computer parallel printer port LPT1, and an HP LaserJet, configured to print to a disc file. Your selections will, obviously, not be the same.

Best printed output results are usually obtained when using a laser printer. So, if you want to produce high-quality documents, and you have access to a laser printer (even if it is not connected to your computer and does not itself have access to Ami Pro), then install the laser printer as an additional printer to be used with Windows and configure it to print to 'File', as shown here.

To install an extra printer press the **Add** button in the 'Printers' dialogue box, choose a printer from the list displayed, and select **Install**. Each time you choose to install a different printer, Windows will ask you to insert a particular disc in the A: drive, so that the appropriate printer driver (a file containing the instructions Windows needs to control that printer) can be copied to your computer's hard disc. Then use the 'Connect' dialogue box to select the print destination, as shown above.

Next, reactivate Ami Pro and use the **File, Printer Setup** command and highlight the printer you want to use in the 'Select Printer' dialogue box, as shown here.

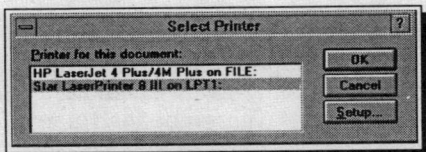

From this dialogue box you can select the default printer or any other installed printer. Next, press **Setup,** select the paper size and orientation needed, and then either press **OK** to confirm your selection, or **Cancel** to abort the procedure.

Now your printer is set up you can, at any time, use the **File, Print** command from the Ami Pro menu bar, or <Ctrl+P>, or mouse click the **Print** SmartIcon, all of which open the 'Print' box, shown here.

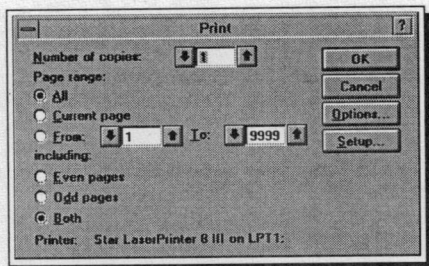

The settings in this box allow you to select the number of copies, and which pages, you want printed. The **Options** button gives you access to some more advanced print options, such as printing in reverse order, or with and without notes, pictures or document descriptions. The **Setup** option gives you another chance to alter your printer settings, before finally selecting **OK**, to send print output from Ami Pro to your selection, either the printer connected to your computer, or to an encoded file on disc.

Printing from a File:

An encoded print file, as described above, has all the printer commands embedded in it and can be printed on, for example, a laser printer by using the simple DOS command

```
COPY Filename LPT1 /B
```

to copy the file to the printer, from the computer connected to it. Ami Pro, or indeed Windows, do not need to be running, or even installed, on this computer at all. The /B is required to tell the printer to expect a binary file (with embedded printer commands), not just a text file.

Do remember that, whenever you change printers, the appearance of your document may change, as Ami Pro uses the fonts available with the newly selected printer. This can affect the line lengths, which in turn will affect both tabulation and pagination of your document.

6. PAGE LAYOUTS AND RULERS

Page Layout in Ami Pro

Page layout includes all page formatting information. The standard page layout is included in the style sheet that you select when you create a document, with the **File**, **New** command. Each page in a document can have only one layout and this includes settings for:

- Left, right, top, and bottom margins
- Left, right, centre, numeric, and leader tabs
- The number of columns, and the gutter width, or the space between each column
- Page size and orientation
- Headers or footers
- Which pages in the document to use the settings on
- Placement and style of lines around page and between columns.

Because every document in Ami Pro has to be based on a Style Sheet which includes the standard page layout for the document, you must either modify a standard layout, or insert a new one, in order to make any changes. You cannot create one from scratch.

Modifying a Page Layout

As long as you are in Layout mode you can easily modify a page layout. You can change the standard page layout settings for your entire document, insert a new page layout, or revert to the standard page layout again. When the page layout is altered, Ami Pro automatically reformats the document using that layout. Any changes you make are effective only for the current document, unless you save the page layout to the existing, or a new, style sheet. Remember that when Ami Pro creates a style sheet only the first page layout in the current document is saved to it.

To understand page layouts you must understand the 'Modify Page Layout' boxes shown on the next few pages. Create a new document, with the default style, and open the dialogue box with the **Page**, **Modify Page Layout** command.

Another way to quickly open this box is to click the right mouse button when the mouse pointer is in any margin area of the page.

This dialogue box has 5 major display areas; one for each of the main modification options shown in the top left 'sub-box'. The initial display option, shown on the next page, is for modifying margins and columns, but we choose to sort out the printer paper layout first. Click on the **Page settings** button to get the dialogue box shown below.

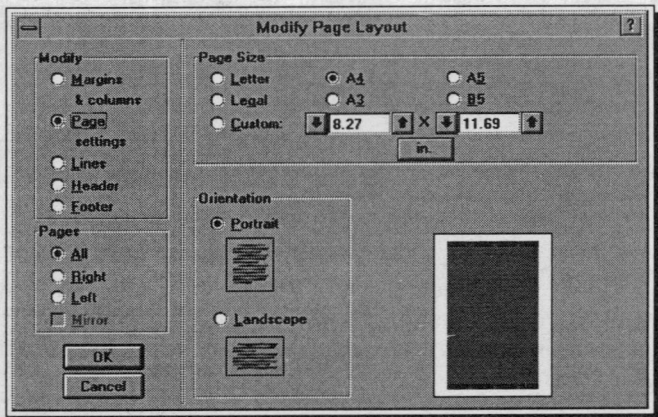

Modifying Page Settings:
The default paper size is A4, but you can change it to:

Letter	8.5 in. x 11 in.
Legal	8.5 in. x 14 in.
A3	29.70 cm x 41.99 cm
A4	21.00 cm x 29.69 cm
A5	14.80 cm x 21.00 cm
B5	17.60 cm x 25.00 cm
Custom	To create a custom page of up to 22 x 22 inches.

Check that the paper size matches that in your printer, otherwise you may get strange results. The other setting you need to decide on is the **Orientation**. If you select **Portrait**, text prints across the page width, while **Landscape** prints across the page length. Usually, only laser printers can print in landscape.

Modifying Margins and Columns:

The initial settings box, shown below, lets you control the number of columns on your page, as well as their size and separation, your paper margins (the blank areas around the edges) and to set various types of tab markers.

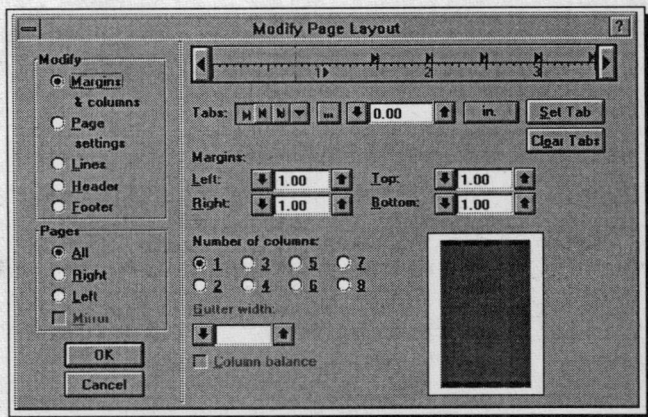

The sample 'page' in the bottom right of the dialogue boxes shows, where relevant, how your changes will look on a real page. Click on one of the **Number of columns** buttons to see how the 'page' box changes. Now change the **Gutter width** to see how to set the separation zones between columns. You can also change column widths and separation, by dragging the black triangle pointers in the bottom half of the ruler with your mouse pointer. Try this as well. When you let one go, by releasing the mouse button, the page box display will immediately update.

In Ami Pro you can use 4 different units for setting page measurements. The default is inches. Click on the **'in.'** button under the ruler, it will change through centimetres, picas and points. Note that all the dimension numbers in the box are immediately updated whenever you make a change to the units.

Page Layout Tabs:

You can create up to 22 'Tab Settings' in Ami Pro and they will show on the top of the ruler, coloured blue. The default ruler is 8.3 inches long, but this will obviously change depending on the width of page you have specified. To see its hidden length just click on the arrow buttons at either end. To clear the ruler of tab settings press the **Clear Tabs** button. The easiest way to set a tab is to click on the tab type button (from left to right the buttons are Left, Right, Numeric, Centre and Leader Character) and then click your mouse pointer in the top half of the scale where you want to set the tab. The tab types available are:

Left   Left aligns the text after the tab.

Right   Right aligns the text after the tab. Displays typed characters to the left of the tab setting.

Numeric   Displays typed characters to the left of the tab setting until a numeric separator is typed, the remaining characters then display to the right of the tab setting. The numeric separator is determined by the Number Format specified in the Windows Control Panel (see Chapter 3).

Centre   Positions text evenly to the left and right of the tab setting.

If you want tabular text to be separated by a character instead of by spaces, click the Leader Character button in the tab bar until the desired leader character displays on the Tab button. The options are underline, dashed, dotted or none (the default). The Contents and Index pages of this book are set with right tabs and dotted leader characters.

To create a tab in a precise position, you can type the position for the tab in the text box, or press the up or down arrows, and then choose the **Set Tab** button.

Setting Page Lines:

You can place lines around part, or all, of the page, or between columns for all of your document - the Index at the back of this book was produced as a document with two columns and a line separating them. Select **Lines** from the 'Modify Page Layout' box to open the dialogue box shown at the top of the next page. In this box you can select **All**, **Left**, **Right**, **Top**, or **Bottom** to specify where your lines should display. Leave them all blank if you don't want any lines.

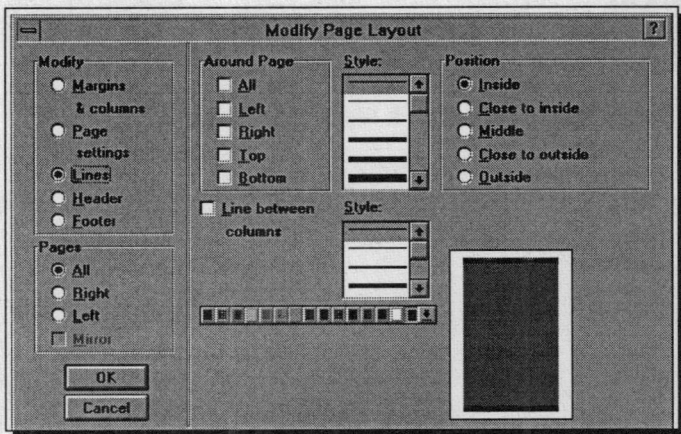

You have the option to select a line's Colour, Style and Position. The line positions are placed between a margin and the edge of the page and are set as follows:

Inside Displays the line you selected *on* the corresponding margin.

Close to inside Displays the line *just outside* the corresponding margin.

Middle	Displays the line *halfway between* the margin and the edge of the paper.
Close to outside	Displays the line *just inside* the corresponding edge of the paper.
Outside	Displays the line *on* the corresponding edge of the paper.

Note that if lines set to **Outside,** or **Close to outside,** do not print, they may be in the 'no print' area for your printer, especially if it is a laser. You may have to select **Middle** to get them to print.

Header and Footer Format:

You can specify separate page formats for both the headers and footers you may want to type in the top, or bottom, margins of your document. The 'Header' dialogue box is shown below.

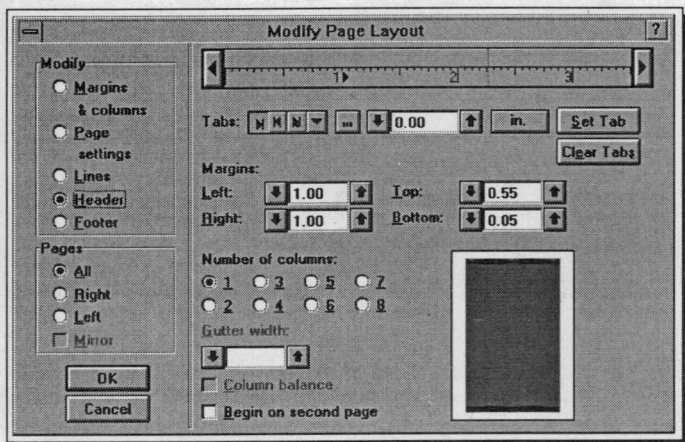

All the selection options are the same as those described in the **Margins and Columns** section, so they will not be repeated here. Any changes you make will show in the two darker bands of the 'sample page' of the dialogue box.

Finally, you can specify whether you want the page layout you have modified to apply to all the pages in the document, or to only its right, or left pages. If you choose right, or left pages, you can select to have them mirrored, which uses the same page layout settings on both the left and right pages, but reverses them. This is sometimes called a 'facing pages' layout.

Inserting a Page Layout

An Ami Pro page can contain only one page layout, so if you insert a new layout, the program inserts a page break at the insertion point and reformats the remainder of the document with the settings of your new page layout, or until it encounters another inserted page layout, or a revert to standard page layout command.

To insert a page layout place the cursor on the position where you want the new layout to begin, select **Page**, **Insert Page Layout**, followed by **Insert**, and specify the desired settings for the new page layout, as described in this chapter. When finished press **OK** to place an inserted page layout mark on the last line of the preceding page. To display this page layout mark, choose **View**, **View Preferences** and select **Marks**.

You can remove a page layout mark by placing the cursor anywhere in the text using the inserted page layout, choosing **Page**, **Insert Page Layout** and then **Remove**. If **Remove** is dimmed, it means that the cursor is not located on a page using an inserted page layout.

If you had selected **Revert**, in the above procedure, Ami Pro would have changed back to the standard page layout from the cursor position, without you having to specify any settings in the 'Modify Page Layout' dialogue box.

Tabs and Rulers in Ami Pro

In Ami Pro, tabs, and sometimes column controls, are set in rulers; you can set tabs in text, in text frames, in tables and for all main document text regardless of the paragraph styles assigned to that text.

Tabs can be set in several ways within a document. As we have seen they can be set in Page Layouts. They can be set for each paragraph style in the 'Modify Style' dialogue box, or for a text frame in the 'Modify Frame Layout' dialogue box. Also if you are in Layout mode you can specify tabs, columns and indentions in the current ruler displayed at the top of the screen.

Note: Ami Pro gives rulers a priority order. Paragraph style rulers override the page layout ruler, but the current ruler overrides both the others.

The Current Ruler:

To display the current ruler across the top of the screen, press **View**, **Show Ruler**. If you point and click on this, the tab buttons are brought up as shown below. This should, by now, be familiar.

A current ruler shows the tab settings, indentions, left and right margins, and number of columns which are in effect at

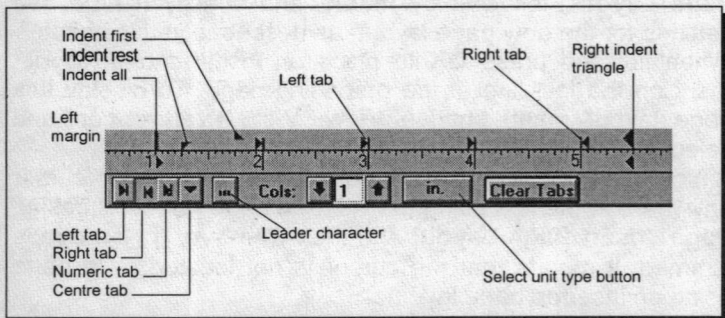

the cursor location. If you want to change any of these settings for the current paragraph, or for selected text, you can insert a new ruler in two ways. The easiest is to click on the current ruler, make your changes and click back on the text. A new ruler mark will be inserted at the beginning of the paragraph, or selected text. You can also insert a new ruler with the **Page**, **Ruler**, **Insert** commands, modify the ruler settings and then click on the text to insert the ruler mark and remove the button bar, as before. You can display ruler marks by choosing **View**, **View Preferences** and selecting **Marks**.

To clear the ruler of tab settings press the **Clear Tabs** button. The easiest way to set a tab is to click on the tab type button (from left to right the buttons are Left, Right, Numeric, Centre and Leader Character) and then click your mouse pointer in the top half of the scale where you want to set the tab. Tabs can be dragged along the ruler to reposition them, or dragged off the ruler to remove them.

To modify indentions in the current ruler, place the insertion point in the paragraph where you want to modify the indention, or select the desired text and click in the current ruler displayed at the top of the screen. If you want to modify the indention for all lines in a paragraph, position the mouse pointer on the 'Indent all' solid line in the top half of the ruler and drag the line to the desired position. To alter the indentions of the first line, or the rest, of the paragraph drag the 'Indent first', or 'Indent rest', triangle buttons respectively, to the required location.

An inserted ruler mark is placed at the beginning of the current paragraph. Any changes you make to a ruler affect only the current paragraph. However, if you press <Enter> to begin a new paragraph, Ami Pro inserts a new ruler with the same settings as the previous one.

To remove an inserted ruler follow the same procedure as for removing an inserted page layout described earlier. Place the cursor anywhere in the text which is using the inserted ruler, choose **Page**, **Ruler** and then **Remove**.

7. USING PARAGRAPH STYLES

We have mentioned previously, in Chapter 4, the importance of Styles and Style sheets in Ami Pro, but we have confined ourselves to using the default style only. In this chapter we will get to grips with how styles can be used, created, modified and how style sheets can be managed.

As mentioned, a style sheet can consist of three main components:

- It contains a page layout, which controls the initial page formatting of your document; as we learned in the last chapter the style page format can be overruled in a particular document.

- It contains a series of paragraph styles to control the initial paragraph formatting. By using these styles you can format your document paragraphs both consistently and very rapidly. You can overrule any style formatting in an individual paragraph however, by manual text formatting.

- A style sheet can also contain text, frames and graphics, which you can use whenever you use that style sheet to create a document. You could, for example, include your company logo and address in a customised style sheet. It would then always be available. If your printer was suitable, you could in fact produce your own headed paper in this way and save a considerable amount of money.

Ami Pro Standard Style Sheets

When Ami Pro was installed on your computer the Setup program should have opened a subdirectory named STYLES and placed in it the standard style sheets provided with the package. There are over 50 of these and each one is saved in a separate file with a name similar to '_default.sty'. The listing on the next page shows them all, with a short description of each one.

If you have not already done so, check on the default directories Ami Pro uses to find its non system files. Press **Tools**, **User Setup** and select **Paths** to see where your document, backup, SmartIcon and macro files, as well as your style sheets, are stored. If you want, you can change any of these settings.

File/Directory:	Description:
_AMIENV.STY	Envelope - Used for automatic envelope printing
_ARTICLE.STY	Article - paragraph styles for professional publications
_BASIC.STY	Basic - Body Text & Body Single paragraph styles
_CALDAY.STY	Calendar - daily by half hour, with to do list
_CALMON.STY	Monthly Calendar format. Select With contents.
_CALORG.STY	Calendar - monthly, from Lotus Organizer
_CALWK.STY	Calendar - weekly by hour, with to do list
_DEFAULT.STY	Default - most frequently used paragraph styles
_DISSERT.STY	Dissertation - paragraph styles for theses and dissertations
_ENVELOP.STY	Envelope - with return address area
_ESSAY.STY	Essay - paragraph styles for research papers
_EXPENSE.STY	Expense Report - with self-totaling columns and rows
_FAX1.STY	Fax - plain, without borders
_FAX2.STY	Fax - with large black top border
_FAX3.STY	Fax - with fill pattern in top border
_HANDOUT.STY	Handout - created based on Freelance for Windows
_INDEX.STY	Index - used every time you create an index
_INVOICE.STY	Invoice - with self-totaling columns
_LABEL.STY	Label - compatible with Avery® laser labels
_LETTER1.STY	Letter - business, with globe graphic
_LETTER2.STY	Letter - business, with border around page
_LETTER3.STY	Letter - business, informal with company name
_LETTER4.STY	Letter - business, with company name
_LOANPAY.STY	Create a loan payment table based on minimum and maximum loan amounts.
_MACRO.STY	Macro sheet - Suggested when writing macros
_MEMO1.STY	Memo - informal, with line down left margin
_MEMO2.STY	Memo - informal, with Memo text in grey frame
_MEMO3.STY	Memo - informal, with line above Memorandum text
_MEMO4.STY	Memo - informal, with sawtooth graphic across top of page
_MEMO5.STY	Memo - informal, with Memo text & grey bar across top of page
_MEMO6.STY	Memo - informal, with diamond graphic across top of page
_MERGDAT.STY	Merge data file - with merge field names and delimiters
_MERGLET.STY	Merge letter - _LETTER1.STY with merge fields
_NEWSLT1.STY	Newsletter - 2-column, with frames for graphics
_NEWSLT2.STY	Newsletter - 1-column, with title in frame with fill pattern
_NEWSLT3.STY	Newsletter - 3-column, with frames for graphics
_NEWSLT4.STY	Newsletter - 3-column, with frame for graphic
_NEWSLT5.STY	Newsletter - 2-column, with fountain pen graphic
_OUTLIN1.STY	Outline - most frequently used outline paragraph styles
_OUTLIN2.STY	Outline - with large left margin & line across top of page
_OUTLIN3.STY	Outline - with large left margin for notes
_OUTLINE.STY	Outline - used in Outline mode
_OVERHD1.STY	Overhead - portrait orientation, with number graphic
_OVERHD2.STY	Overhead - landscape orientation, with arrow graphic
_OVERHD3.STY	Overhead - landscape orientation, with starburst graphic
_OVERHD4.STY	Overhead - simple, with 8.5" x 8.5" page size
_OVERHD5.STY	Overhead - with top line, with 8.5" x 8.5" page size
_PHONLST.STY	Phone list - 2-column, with first & last name & phone # fields
_PRESS1.STY	Press Release - with lines above & below heading
_PRESS2.STY	Press Release - with news release graphic
_PROPOS1.STY	Proposal - simple, with line above & below
_PROPOS2.STY	Proposal - 2-column, with categories in frames
_REPORT1.STY	Report - simple, with line under title
_REPORT2.STY	Report - 2-column, with sections
_REPORT3.STY	Report - 2-column, with title in frame spanning columns
_REPORT4.STY	Report - 1-column with categories in frames
_TERMPPR.STY	Term Paper - paragraph styles for research papers
_TITLE1.STY	Title Page - formal, frame has shadow border
_TITLE2.STY	Title Page - formal, frame has double-lined border
_TITLE3.STY	Title Page - informal, frame has grey background
_TOC.STY	Table of Contents - used every time you create a TOC

Directory: c:\amipro\styles

Ami Pro File Manager — File View Help

[..]
[-a-]
[-c-]
[-d-]
[-e-]
[+]
[+]

The 'Style Sheet Guide', shipped with Ami Pro 3, gives a little information on the standard style sheets and shows a sample print out of each one. It is well worth spending a couple of hours exploring the standard styles. To do this open a new file, with the **File**, **New** command and study the dialogue box produced, an example of which was shown on page 28. It is in this box that you determine what style sheet a document will be linked to. If **List by description** is checked the style list will make more sense to you. If you select **Close current file** the new file opened will replace the current file, but you will be given the chance to save it if it has been altered since last saved.

To get a feel for the power of these style sheets try loading the Monthly Calendar (_calmon.sty), but make sure that you first check the **With contents** and **Run macro** boxes. These will ensure that the style contents text will be loaded into the opened file and that any embedded macro will be run and will prompt you for information to use in the 'document'.

The macro opens a dialogue box to let you choose the month and year wanted and has the current ones for the system clock already selected. It will then build a one sheet calendar for the month selected, similar to the following:

1994	November					1994
Sunday	Monday	Tuesday	Wednesday	Thursday	Friday	Saturday
			1	2	3	4	5
6	7	8	9	10	11	12
13	14	15	16	17	18	19
20	21	22	23	24	25	26
27	28	29	30			

You can enter text anywhere on the calendar sheet, which is in fact built in a large Ami Pro table. The best way to navigate round it, we think, is to click your mouse on the date cell you want to work with and use the 'Toggle full page/layout view' SmartIcon to rapidly magnify the working area. This icon is on most of the available SmartIcon bars.

We are sure you will find many uses for the three calendars that Ami Pro will automatically produce using these style sheets. In fact the style macros go further with the weekly and daily ones. A 'Default Information' dialogue box is opened, as shown below, for you to add personal information which it stores and uses to customise some of the sheets.

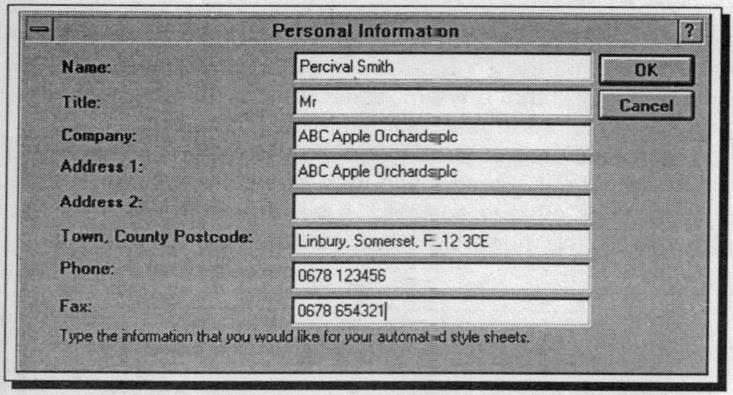

Personal Information		?
Name:	Percival Smith	OK
Title:	Mr	Cancel
Company:	ABC Apple Orchards plc	
Address 1:	ABC Apple Orchards plc	
Address 2:		
Town, County Postcode:	Linbury, Somerset, F_12 3CE	
Phone:	0678 123456	
Fax:	0678 654321	

Type the information that you would like for your automated style sheets.

In Ami Pro 3.0 the data you type into this box can prove difficult to get rid of, so don't type personal information that you may not want to see on the screen every time you use the style sheet. If you do ever want to delete, or edit, the saved default information, it is stored in the file **AMIPRO2.INI** in the Windows working directory, under the section titled [AutoStyleSheets], as shown below:

```
[AutoStyleSheets]
NoQuestions=0
DataGood=1
Name=Percival Smith
```

```
Title=Mr
Company=ABC Apple Orchards plc
Address1=ABC Apple Orchards plc
Address2=
CSZ=Linbury, Somerset, PL12 3CE
Phone=0678 123456
Fax=0678 654321
```

This can easily be edited with the Windows Notepad. Ami Pro 3.1 includes the macro **collect.smm**, which you can run to make this task easier.

A second dialogue box is opened by the macro, giving you the option to edit the text for the new document and, if you want to make it a permanent part of every document using the style sheet, to **Save As** a new style sheet. Finally, the macro adds your name, company and address, etc., to produce a heading as shown in the example below.

Another one to look at quickly is the **'_letter1.sty'** style sheet. If you use this to open a new document you will be given options to edit your personal details and to enter those for the letter recipient. You are then presented with a beautifully laid out business letter which only requires entry of the body text. There are even embedded notes to help you out. This letter format may be too formal for some uses, in which case try the others out. Once you find the format you like, with very little modification, you can customise it to your own needs.

Some of the included style sheets do not have contents or macros, these contain suitable paragraph styles for text formatting. You have to enter text into these generated document 'shells' before you can test out the paragraph styles provided.

Manipulating Style Sheets

You could go through life just using Ami Pro's standard style sheets without producing any of your own, but with a little practice and patience, you can generate your own styles and get much more out of the program.

To demonstrate some procedures we will use the file PCUSERS3.SAM, which was produced and hopefully saved, in a previous chapter. Open the file, which was, if you remember, created using the '_default' style.

Style Basics:

When a file is first created it has access to all the individual paragraph styles included in the attached style sheet. Any other document using the same style sheet can also use these same paragraph styles. Hence the possibility of standardising formats across all your documents.

As we learned in a previous chapter you can override a style by manually formatting all, or part, of your text. This procedure alters the text in that document but does not alter the information in the style sheet itself. You can, if you wish, create a new paragraph style, define, or modify, an existing one in a specific document. These actions, as we shall see, initially produce styles which are then specific to that document only, and are embedded in it. To see this, select **Style**, **Style Management** to open the dialogue box on the next page.

This Style Management box lists all the styles available to the current document and we will come back to it later. As you can see there are two lists of styles; those in the style sheet on the right, and those in the document on the left. In

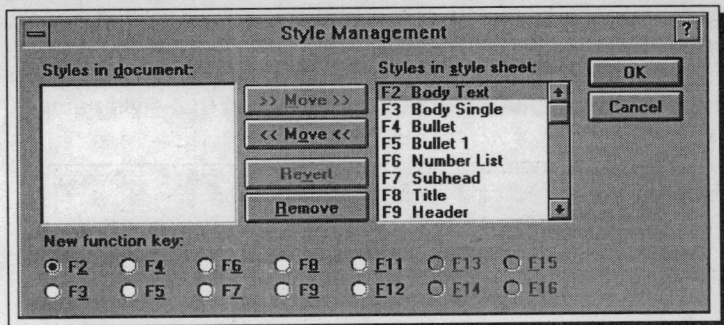

Style Management

Styles in document:

Styles in style sheet:
- F2 Body Text
- F3 Body Single
- F4 Bullet
- F5 Bullet 1
- F6 Number List
- F7 Subhead
- F8 Title
- F9 Header

OK
Cancel

>> Move >>
<< Move <<
Revert
Remove

New function key:
- F2 F4 F6 F8 F11 F13 F15
- F3 F5 F7 F9 F12 F14 F16

our case we have not produced any document styles yet, so the list on the left is empty. Press **Cancel** to remove the dialogue box.

Defining a Style:

In the file PCUSERS3.SAM, highlight the subheading text 'Personal Computers' and look at the Style Status button at the bottom of the screen. It should show as **Subhead**. Now manually reformat the highlighted text. Select **Text, Font** and choose Arial of 12 point size (or another font if this one is not available to your printer). Underline the still selected text with the **Text, Underline** commands, or by clicking on the 'Underline text' SmartIcon, or with the <Ctrl+U> key strokes. The text should now be reformatted on screen, but the Style Status button should still be the same.

As this text is now in the format we want to use for all our future subheadings we will make it into a style, so select **Style, Define Style**. This warning message will result which

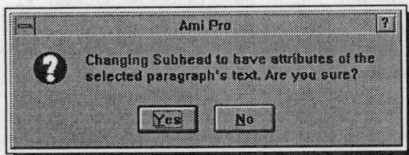

Ami Pro

Changing Subhead to have attributes of the selected paragraph's text. Are you sure?

Yes   No

gives you the chance to change your mind before overwriting the old 'Subhead' style in the document. Select 'Yes' to continue. Now if you look at the Style

Status button a small round bullet should show before the name, as follows, '·Subhead'. This tells you that 'Subhead' is now a document style and, at the moment, only available to this particular document. Open the 'Style Management' box again to confirm this; it should be the same as that shown below.

The **Define Style** command, when implemented, reformats all of the text in the current document using that style name.

Creating a Style:

In a previous chapter we spent some time manually creating some hanging indents in the penultimate four paragraphs of our document PCUSERS3.SAM. We will now generate a style from this previous work. Place the cursor in one of these paragraphs, maybe in the 'Name Description' line, select **Style, Create Style**, and make the changes shown here to the dialogue box. When this has been done select **Create** and a new style 'Temp Margin 1' will be created from the formatting details of the first word in the selected paragraph (the one in which the cursor was placed).

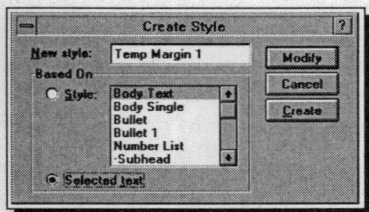

Note that the **Create Style** command has not changed the style of any document text, but it has added a new style to the list of ones available in the document. It also has a bullet in front of its name in the list, indicating a document style.

Highlight the four paragraphs with hanging indents and change their style to the new 'Temp Margin 1', by clicking the mouse in the Style Button list, as shown on the next page.

80

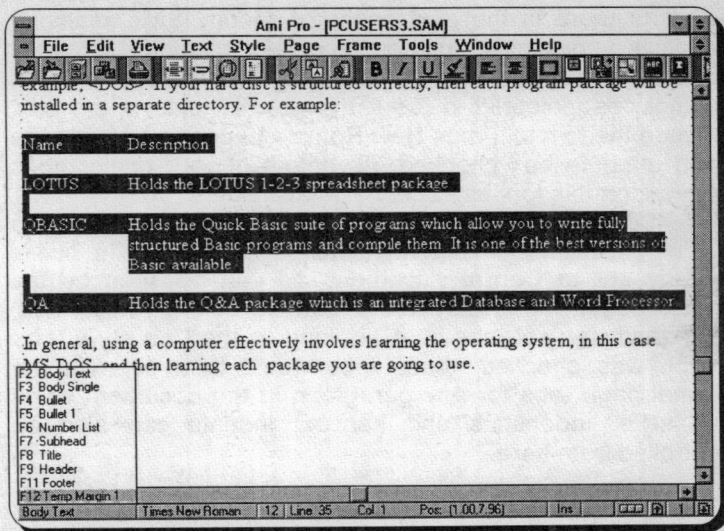

```
━━━━━━━━━━━━━━━━━━━━━━━━━━━━━━━━━━━━━━━━━━━━━━━━━━━━━━━━━━━
                    Ami Pro - [PCUSERS3.SAM]
  File  Edit  View  Text  Style  Page  Frame  Tools  Window  Help
```

example, <DOS. If your hard disc is structured correctly, then each program package will be
installed in a separate directory. For example:

Name	Description
LOTUS	Holds the LOTUS 1-2-3 spreadsheet package
QBASIC	Holds the Quick Basic suite of programs which allow you to write fully structured Basic programs and compile them. It is one of the best versions of Basic available.
QA	Holds the Q&A package which is an integrated Database and Word Processor

In general, using a computer effectively involves learning the operating system, in this case
MS-DOS, and then learning each package you are going to use.

```
F2 Body Text
F3 Body Single
F4 Bullet
F5 Bullet 1
F6 Number List
F7 Subhead
F8 Title
F9 Header
F11 Footer
F12 Temp Margin 1
```
Body Text   Times New Roman   12 Line 35   Col 1   Pos: (1.00,7.96)   Ins

Modifying Styles:
The third way of generating paragraph styles is to modify
some of the properties of an existing style and save the new
style under a different name. This procedure is also used to
alter the characteristics of a style, whilst retaining its name.

We will modify the title style first, so place the cursor in the
title line of PCUSERS3.SAM and activate the **Style**, **Modify
Style** menu commands, which will open the box below.

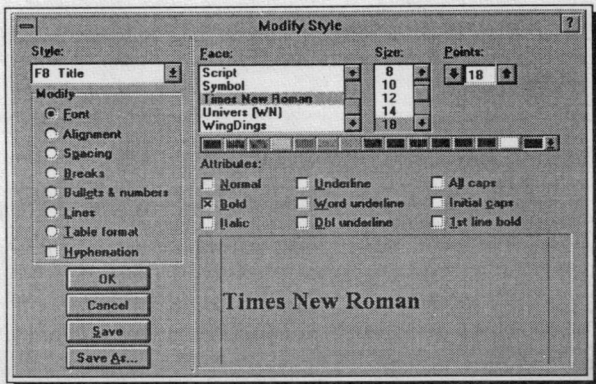

The procedure in the next series of 'Modify Style' dialogue boxes is very similar to that described for modifying page layouts. The initial box displayed is for changing **Font** settings, as indicated in the list on the left side of the box. Change the font to Times New Roman 18 point and leave the **Bold** attribute box checked. As before, if your printer does not support this font use one that is available to you.

Next click on the **Alignment** button to open the box shown below. We will not change any settings in this box. The title is already set to **Centre** alignment, as can be seen by the middle paragraph display in the 'sample' box. If you wanted, you could also set tabs here. As long as the **Use style tabs** button was checked, these tabs would then override the normal page tabs for any paragraph in the document using this style. Indentions and hanging indents can also be controlled from here.

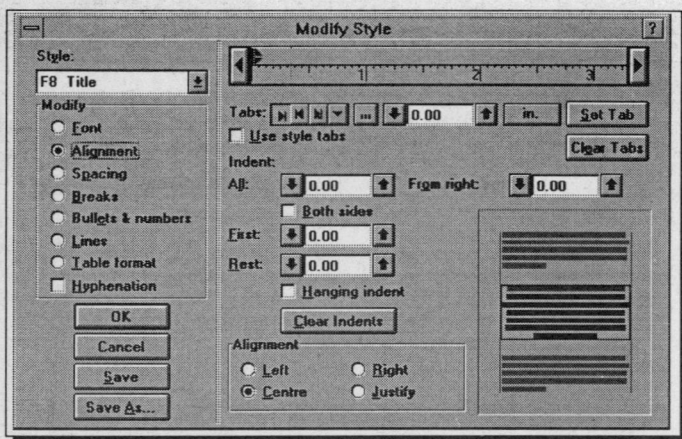

Click on the **Spacing** button to open the next dialogue box, shown on the facing page. The Spacing box allows you to control line spacing and text tightness within individual paragraphs. Paragraph spacing lets you force blank space **Above** and **Below** the paragraph. With these both set to zero there would be no extra spacing included around your paragraph.

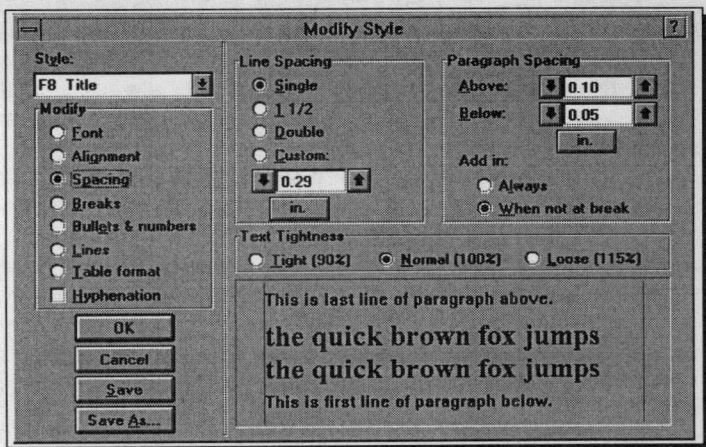

Modify Style

Style: F8 Title

Modify
- Font
- Alignment
- ● Spacing
- Breaks
- Bullets & numbers
- Lines
- Table format
- ☐ Hyphenation

OK
Cancel
Save
Save As...

Line Spacing
- ● Single
- 1 1/2
- Double
- Custom: 0.29 in.

Paragraph Spacing
- Above: 0.10
- Below: 0.05 in.

Add in:
- Always
- ● When not at break

Text Tightness
- Tight (90%)
- ● Normal (100%)
- Loose (115%)

This is last line of paragraph above.

the quick brown fox jumps
the quick brown fox jumps

This is first line of paragraph below.

The shown setting places a 0.1 inch space above the paragraph, but not if this would appear at the top of a page, as the **When not at break** button is checked.

The best way to find out how these work is to change the selections and see the effect of each on the sample text. Make sure, this time, that you return the settings to those shown, as we do not want to make any changes.

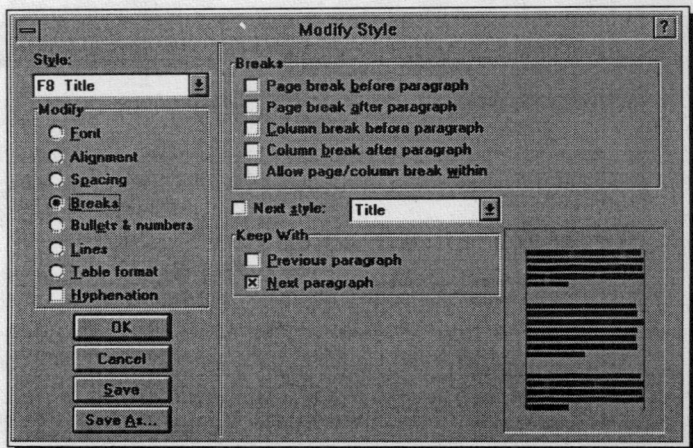

Modify Style

Style: F8 Title

Modify
- Font
- Alignment
- Spacing
- ● Breaks
- Bullets & numbers
- Lines
- Table format
- ☐ Hyphenation

OK
Cancel
Save
Save As...

Breaks
- ☐ Page break before paragraph
- ☐ Page break after paragraph
- ☐ Column break before paragraph
- ☐ Column break after paragraph
- ☐ Allow page/column break within

☐ Next style: Title

Keep With
- ☐ Previous paragraph
- ☒ Next paragraph

The **Breaks** box, on the previous page, allows you to force page, or column, breaks before and after paragraphs set with this style. You could select **Next style** if you always follow one style with another; for example, if you always use the Body Text style after a Title, you could check this box and select Body Text in the pull-down window.

Our example shows the **Keep with**, **Next paragraph** box selected, to force titles to stay 'attached' to their following text.

Now select the **Lines** button, as we are going to make some changes in this box, as shown below.

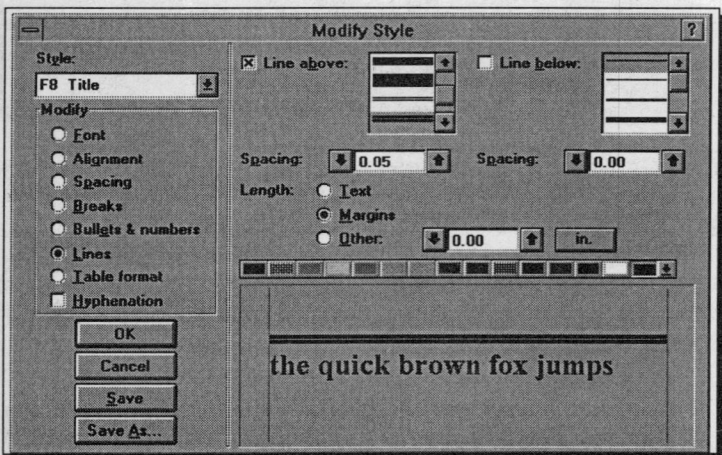

This is a simple box which allows you to place lines, of various type and length, above and/or below paragraphs with the style. In the selection shown we have placed a double line above the Title paragraphs to fit between the page margins, with 0.05 inches above the text.

We have now finished modifying the Title style, so **Save** it and select 'Bullet 1', from the **Style** pull-down window in the top left corner. If you had forgotten to save the changes made to the 'Title' style, a warning box would have reminded you.

Now select the **Bullets & numbers** button to open the box on the facing page.

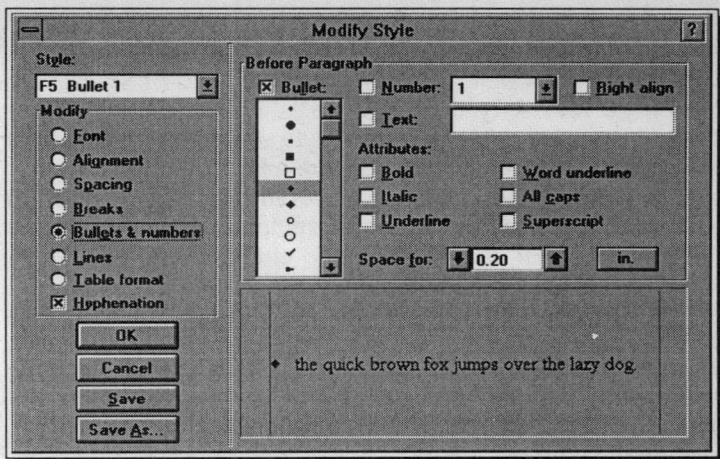

This allows you to select bullets, numbers and strings of leading text to start the first line of the paragraph. You will need to experiment a little with these settings, but the important rule is that you select, and enter text into, the various boxes in the order that you want the selections, or 'leader' text, to print. An example of how your selection will look is always shown in the 'sample' box.

There are several examples of bullet and numbered list styles in the provided style sheets, including '_default.sty'. If you find one you like, examine its settings, as we have done here, and incorporate them into your own style sheets.

As a final exercise for you to carry out on your own, change the font **Face** of all the paragraph styles to Arial. Do not forget to **Save** each change, before selecting the next style to modify. When you have completed this select **OK** to see all the changes implemented in your document.

Managing Styles

If you open the 'Styles' box with the commands **Style**, **Select a Style** you will confirm that your document is using the '_default' style and that all the paragraph styles in it now have bullets in front. As we said before this is because all the styles have been modified and are embedded in the

85

document at the moment. At this point you should save your
document with the new name of PCUSERS4.SAM.

Making a New Style Sheet:

As we are going to make a new style sheet, now would be a
good time to make any changes you might need to your page
layout. Maybe your printer uses a different sized paper, or
you want other tab and margin settings. While still in the
present document, make any page changes you decide on,
as described in the last chapter.

It is a simple matter now to create a new style sheet using
all the paragraph styles, and the page layout, of your
document. Select **Style**, **Save as a Style Sheet** and type
pcusers in the **File name** box that is opened. When you
press **OK** the new style sheet '**pcusers.sty**' is created and
attached to your document.

Confirm that this has happened by checking the style
sheet name in the style box. You will also see that all the
styles have now lost their bullets. Save your document again,
this time as PCUSERS5.SAM.

Now let us go back one stage, so open the previous
document PCUSERS4.SAM and select **Style, Style
Management**. The 'Style Management' box should look like
the one below, with all the styles in the document section.

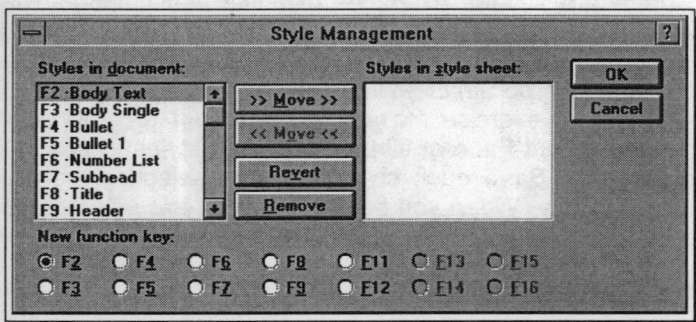

Changing an Existing Style Sheet:

If you decide that some of our modified styles are good
enough to replace the original ones in the '_default' style

86

sheet, you could carry out this operation in the 'Style Management' box.

Select each style from the document side that you want to keep and press the **Move** button, to move it into the style sheet. At the same time you can select what Function key to attach to it. When the right hand box contains the paragraph styles you want in your style sheet (read the WARNING paragraph below), simply select **OK** to save them to the '_default' sheet.

WARNING - this procedure will permanently alter the standard default style sheet. If you wanted it back, you would have to reinstall Ami Pro.

At any stage before selecting **OK** you can select a document style and press **Revert** to cancel any formatting changes made to that paragraph style and cause it to revert to its original state.

Making a Composite Style Sheet:

Using the 'Style Management' box you can build up a style sheet from styles included in other style sheets. To do this, first move any styles you want to keep from the current style sheet into the document. Then use the **Style**, **Use another Style Shee**t command to change the style sheet the document is using and reformat the document. In the 'Style Management' box move any styles you want to keep from this style sheet into the document. Repeat this procedure until you are happy with the styles in the document and then use **Style, Save as a Style Sheet** to create your new sheet.

When first exploring this procedure make sure you have your document saved, especially if it is a long one, as any text in the document linked to a style that does not exist in the other style sheet opened, will be reformatted to Body Text style.

Keeping Format with Document:

When you first **Save** a document, or later change its name with **Save As**, you are given the option to **Keep format with document**, as shown in the dialogue box on page 40. If you leave this option blank the document when next opened will use the style sheet attached to it, and will expect it to be available. If, however, you check this option all the required styles will be embedded in the document, which will no longer need, or be able to use, a style sheet. This procedure is useful if you plan to move the file to another computer and you do not want the bother of moving a style sheet as well; but you will find that you can no longer move the styles back out of the document in the 'Style Management' box.

We are sure that, like us, you will end up saving a file with this option accidentally selected and that the document will no longer react to its usual style sheet. There is an easy way to remedy this situation. Simply create a new temporary style sheet from your document with the **Style, Save as a Style Sheet** command and give the new style sheet a name like **'temp.sty'**. Your document now will have no embedded styles and will be linked to the temporary style. Now you can attach it back to the original style sheet with the command **Style, Use Another Style Sheet**. You should now be able to move styles freely between the document and style sheet.

Special Formatting Features
There are two special features in Ami Pro which force text to override style formatting.

Hard Return:
This forces a new line in a paragraph without actually opening a new paragraph. It is most useful in numbered lists, when you want to have several sections, maybe including blank lines, within one list number. Using <Enter> will start a new paragraph and hence force a new list number. To use a 'Hard return' type <Ctrl+Enter> instead of <Enter>. Try it out with the list style in the '_default' style sheet.

Non-Breaking Space:
If you need to keep two words together in your document and not have them separated by word wrap at the end of a line, you can use the <Ctrl+Spacebar> key strokes to place a non-breaking space between them.

8. USING FRAMES AND DRAWING

Understanding Frames

A frame in Ami Pro is like a 'mini-document' within the main document that allows you to create multiple layouts on the same page. A frame can contain text, or a picture, and is not affected by the formatting of the main document. You can make document text wrap around, flow behind, or flow above and below a frame. A page can contain multiple frames, which can overlap, be transparent or opaque, have lines around them or have a shadow effect.

The main reasons for using frames in your documents are to hold graphics, or drawings, to let you place text outside the normal page layout area (in an indention area or margin, for instance), or to allow you to create a heading to span a multi-column page.

Frames can be moved, or copied, around your document using the same **Edit** commands as ordinary text. The text included in a frame can be formatted manually, or with styles, as in the main document.

Creating a Frame:

To make it easier to create and manipulate frames Ami Pro has come equipped with a Graphics SmartIcon set, which can be accessed by selecting from the list opened when the SmartIcon button is clicked. We also recommend that you use the two rulers provided, when working with frames, so that you can keep track of a frame's size and position on the page. The horizontal ruler is obtained with the **View, Show Ruler** command, and the vertical one obtained by selecting the **Vertical Ruler** option under **View, View Preferences**. If you are not yet familiar with the SmartIcons, right-click your mouse onto each one in turn to find out its purpose.

There are two main ways to create a new frame. Either with the **Frame**, **Create Frame** commands and filling in a dialogue box, or interactively with the mouse. We will assume that you are happy using a mouse and will concentrate on this last method.

Start with a new document and the '_default' style and set up the two rulers as described above. Click your mouse on the 'Add a frame' SmartIcon, position the cross hairs of the frame mouse pointer 4cm from the left margin and 3cm from the top (the pointer position is shown on both rulers by a moving dotted line), hold the left mouse button down and drag the dotted frame until its other corner is at 10cm on the hor. scale and 8cm vertical. This position is shown below.

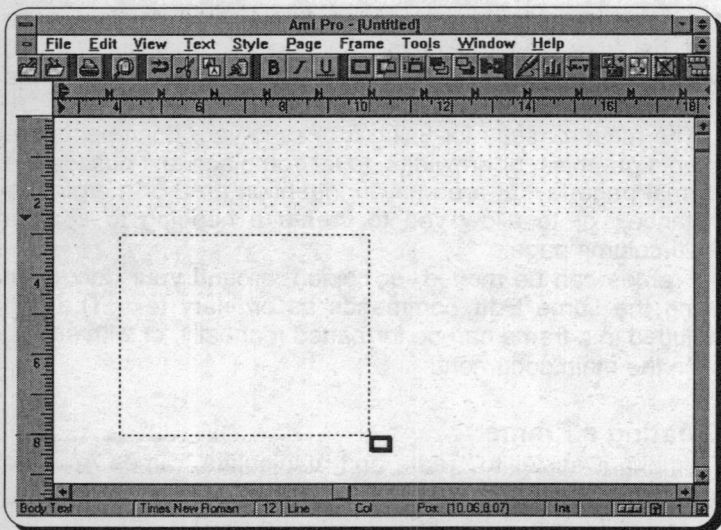

Release the mouse to fix the frame on the page. At the moment it is 'selected', and looks like the top one in the box alongside. The right and bottom lines are thicker because, by default, a frame has a shadow on these sides. The black squares are 'handles', which are used to manipulate the frame. Changes can only be made if a frame is selected. If the mouse is clicked outside the frame it will lose its handles and revert to its normal shape, as shown here on the bottom box alongside. We have produced a

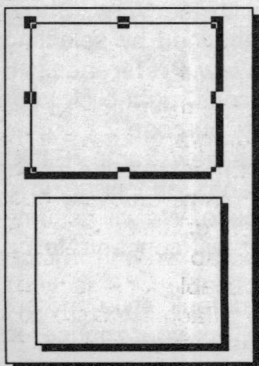

6cm by 5cm rectangular frame with lines all round and shadows on two sides; all of which are easily changeable, as we shall see in the following section.

Modifying Frame Layout:

Click inside the frame again, to select it, and either click the right mouse button, or select the **Frame, Modify frame layout** command to open the following dialogue box.

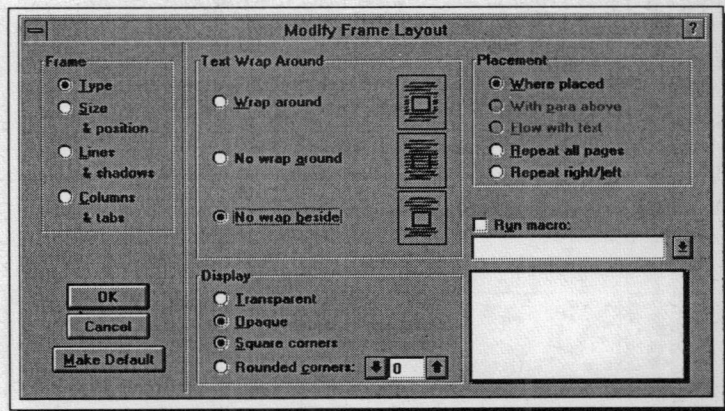

As with the other 'Modify Layout' boxes in Ami Pro, this one has several screens in which to enter your requirements. The first is the **Type** box. The frame is selected with **No wrap beside**, to stay **Where placed** on the page and **Opaque** with **Square corners**. The 'Text Wrap Around' function controls how document text will react with the frame, as shown by the sample sketches alongside the setting buttons.

With the Placement option you can force the frame to stay where you place it, to move with the paragraph above if the document is edited, to flow with the <Enter> marker of the current paragraph, to display exactly the same on every page of the document, or to display on only left, or right, pages. As you select these various options the wrap around choices vary; a grey dimmed option not being available for selection.

The **Run macro** section allows you to attach a macro to a frame. Whenever such a frame is selected, or clicked on, the macro will run. This enables you to design and embed your own icons in a document.

An **Opaque** frame hides anything under its borders, whereas a **Transparent** one allows you to see through it. You can use this feature to layer several frames on top of each other to get quite sophisticated effects.

If you select **Rounded corners** and type a number, between 1 and 100 in the window, you can vary the frame shape between a rectangle and an ellipse (or a circle with a square box). Try this and watch how the sample reacts.

Now open the **Size & position** layout box, shown below, and check how steady your hand was when you placed the frame earlier. The dimensions and positioning should be as shown. If these dimensions are important you can alter them in this box, or you could get Ami Pro to build the frame for you with the **Frame, Create Frame** commands. With this procedure you are prompted to enter all the dimensions. The choice is yours.

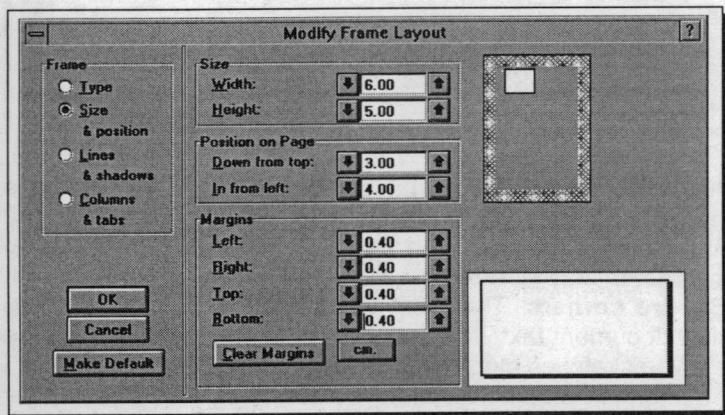

The Margins section allows you to set the total width of margin around the edge of the frame. Select 0.4cm in all four boxes. The grey lines, both inside and outside the black frame lines of the sample display, indicate the area that will be kept blank, both inside and outside of the frame.

If you now select the **Lines & shadows** option, the dialogue box shown below will be displayed. This allows you to set on which sides of the frame, if any, you want lines. If no Lines boxes are checked, your frame will not be surrounded with lines. That way you can use completely invisible frames to help with the overall format of your document pages. **Style** allows you to choose the type of line, while in the Shadow box you can select how much shadow, if any, you want and on what sides of the frame you want it.

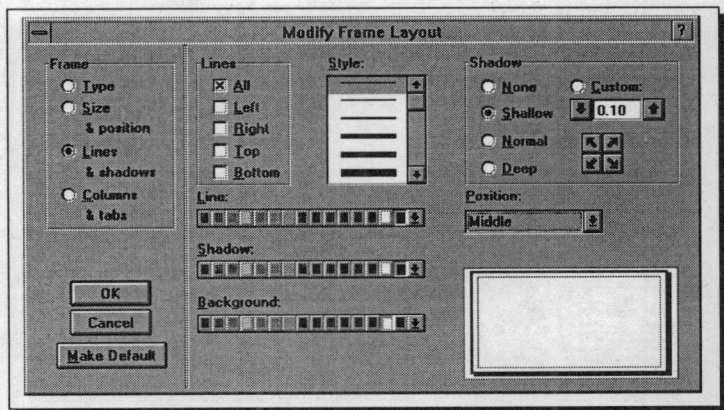

The three colour bars allow you to control the colours of **Lines**, **Shadows** or the frame **Background**. With these you can design some very pretty effects.

The **Position** option is sometimes the most difficult one to come to terms with; it works in conjunction with the Margins selection, described on the previous page. If you select 'Outside', the frame lines will be placed on the outside of the margin area, so all the margin will be inside the frame. If you select 'Inside', the frame lines will be placed on the inside of the margin area, so all the margin will be outside the frame. There are also three intermediate settings. This option is needed to control the distance between document text and the outside of the frame and to 'protect' the frame lines from text inside the frame.

The last 'Modify Frame Layout' box, selected by clicking on the **Columns & tabs** selector is shown below. At this stage of the book this box should need no explanation, as the options available are virtually identical to those for setting a page layout.

With these settings you can treat a frame as a mini-page within a document, with its own column settings and ruler. In this box we have changed the number of columns to 2 to demonstrate this effect later.

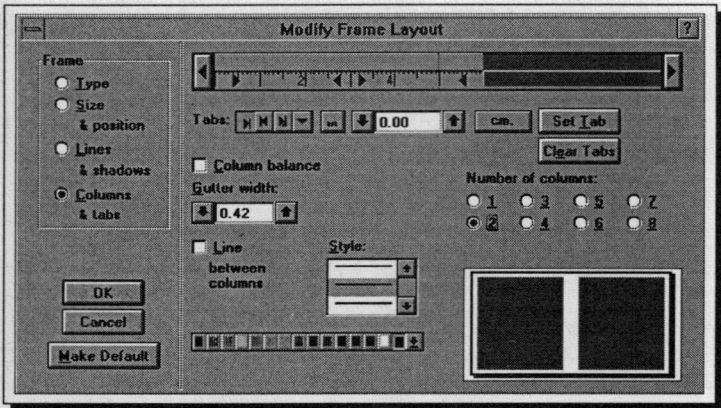

Select **OK** to accept all the settings and in our case to return you to our almost blank page. The frame handles should now be well clear of the lines surrounding it due to the changes we made to the margin settings.

Moving a Frame:

Position the pointer inside the frame, which should still be selected, hold the left mouse button down and drag the frame to any location you want on the page, as shown on the facing page. You in fact drag a dotted frame with the pointer, until you release the mouse button, which then fixes the new frame position.

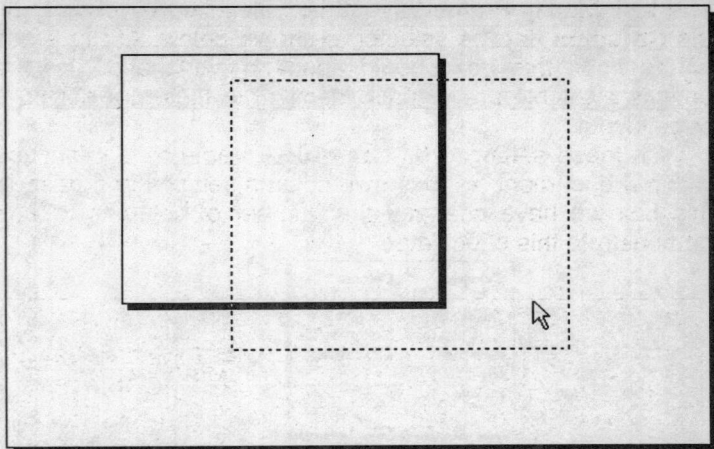

Resizing a Frame:
You use the handles to alter the size and shape of a frame interactively with the mouse. Dragging one of the corner handles will drag the two attached frame sides with the pointer, but dragging a centre line handle will only move that side. Try these actions until you are happy with the resultant frame.

Placing Text in a Frame:
Once you have your frame where you want it on the page it is only of any use if you do something with it, so double click the mouse pointer inside. The handles will turn grey, indicating that they are no longer active, and the cursor will be placed inside the frame ready for you to, either enter text, or process a graphic. Type in some text, but not necessarily the same as we have entered. If you changed the frame settings, as we described, the text should format into two columns as shown on the next page.

When you have finished, click the mouse button outside the frame. This will cancel the frame selection and you will not be able to access, or edit, the text inside the frame until you next double click inside it. Selecting the frame by single

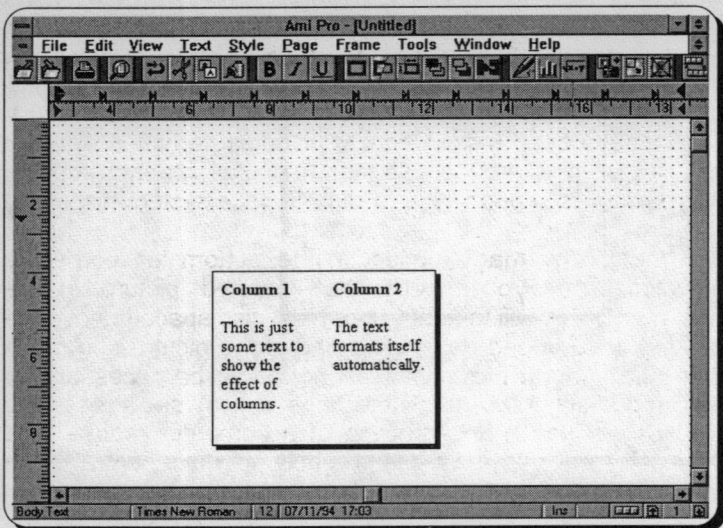

clicking will still let you resize, or move, the frame, but the inside text will not all show if there is not enough room for it.

Importing a Picture into a Frame:

Create another frame on your page and click inside to select it. To import a picture into this frame click on the 'Import picture' Icon, or select the **File, Import Picture** command, either of which will open the dialogue box shown below.

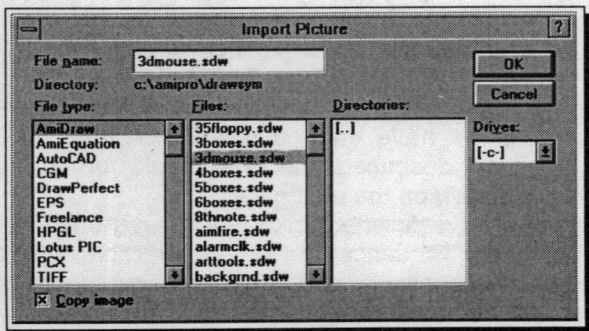

This box allows you to enter the details of the picture, or graphic, that you want to import. The **File type** window gives you the choice of a wide range of graphic formats to import, but we will stick to the Amidraw graphics samples, which should have been loaded onto your computer when Ami Pro was installed. If you chose not to install graphic images, maybe now is a good time to dig out your system discs and remedy this.

If the **Copy image** option, in the bottom left corner, is selected Ami Pro embeds the imported picture in the document. This will take up more hard disc space to save the file, but it will speed up the showing of the picture and mean that the separate picture file will no longer be necessary for this document. Make the selections shown and press **OK**. You should see a line drawing of a computer mouse 'size itself' into your frame. This is probably not quite central in the frame so double click within the frame and see what happens. Ami Pro goes into 'Drawing' mode as shown below.

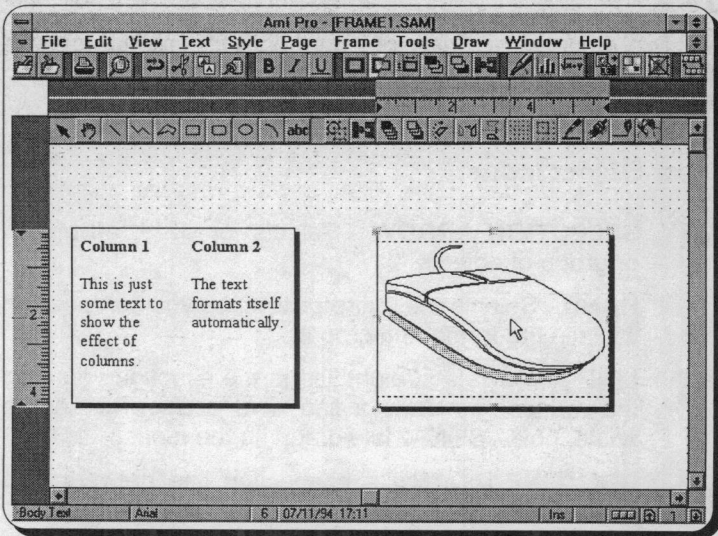

If you click on the graphic you can drag it around inside the frame, but releasing the mouse button fixes its position. Note that you can *crop* a picture in this way, by dragging the section you do not want, so that it is hidden outside of the frame.

The Drawing Tool

As long as you have a mouse, you can use the Ami Pro Drawing function to create, or edit, a picture consisting of lines, arcs, ellipses, and rectangles, but you cannot use a bit-mapped graphic. In Draw mode, you create and select objects in a picture, then copy and move them, or change their size and shape, etc. You cannot, though, create a drawing in a frame that already contains text.

In the Drawing mode, the program displays a new set of icons across the top of the screen, as can be seen in the above illustration. These will be explained in some detail on the next pages.

Using the Draw Icons:

Ami Pro provides a variety of icons, both for creating objects such as lines, circles, or squares and then for manipulating these objects, once they have been selected.

Draw Object Icons:

SELECTION ARROW - Selects, or sizes, an object, or group of objects.

HAND - Selects the entire picture, so you can position it within the frame and crop it.

LINE - Draws a straight line in the direction you drag the mouse. To draw a line at a perfect 45 degree angle, hold <Shift> while dragging the mouse.

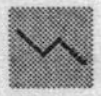

POLYLINE - Draws a connecting line between two points. Click the mouse where you want to start the line, then click the mouse again where you want it to end. The two points are connected.

POLYGON - Draws connecting lines that create the sides of a closed object. Draw each line of the polygon as with Polyline, Ami Pro connects the points and closes the polygon by connecting the first and last points.

RECTANGLE - Draws a rectangle. To draw a square, hold <Shift> and drag the mouse.

ROUNDED RECTANGLE - Draws a rectangle with rounded corners. To draw a rounded square, hold <Shift> and drag the mouse.

ELLIPSE - Draws an ellipse. To draw a circle, hold <Shift> while dragging the mouse.

ARC - Draws an arc. You can create a Bezier curve by modifying an arc.

TEXT - Places the insertion point inside a drawing so you can type text, each paragraph of which will become an object, which you can then manipulate.

Draw Command Icons:

SELECT ALL - Selects, or deselects, all the objects inside the frame.

GROUP/UNGROUP - Groups, or ungroups, the selected objects inside the frame.

BRING TO FRONT - Places the selected object on top of all other objects at that location.

SEND TO BACK - Places the selected object underneath all other objects at that location.

ROTATE - Rotates the selected object, or group of objects, clockwise or anticlockwise.

FLIP HORIZONTALLY - Flips the selected object, or group of objects, from left to right. You can flip any object except a text object.

FLIP VERTICALLY - Flips the selected object, or group of objects, from top to bottom. You can flip any object except a text object.

SHOW/HIDE GRID - Displays, or conceals, a grid inside the frame.

SNAP TO - Aligns objects automatically, or manually, on the grid specified for the frame.

EXTRACT LINE & FILL - Changes the current line style and fill pattern to the line style and fill pattern of the selected object.

APPLY LINE & FILL - Changes the line style and fill pattern of the selected object to the current line style and fill pattern.

LINE STYLE - Displays line style, colour, and various line endings options, such as arrows, etc.

FILL PATTERN - Displays colour and fill pattern options.

Creating a Drawing:

To create an object, click on the object icon required, such as the ellipse, position the mouse pointer where you want to create the object inside the frame and then drag the mouse to draw the object. Hold the <Shift> key while you drag the mouse to create a perfect square, rounded square, or circle. If you do not hold <Shift>, Ami Pro creates a rectangle, rounded rectangle, or ellipse.

You can use the polyline and polygon draw object icons to create freehand objects. Click the polyline or polygon object icon, position the mouse pointer where you want to create the object inside the frame and then hold <Shift> while you drag the mouse. Release the mouse button to stop drawing the object.

Ami Pro creates a text object, using the current 'Draw' mode font, in the upper left corner of the drawing. If the text consists of several paragraphs, Ami Pro creates an object for each paragraph. You can then move the text object(s) to the desired position in the frame.

Editing a Drawing:

To select an object, first click the 'Selection Arrow' icon and then click the desired object. You can select an object that is totally hidden by another object. Hold <Ctrl> and click the top object repeatedly until the desired object is selected. Ami Pro displays black handles around the object selected.

You can move an object, or multiple objects, within a drawing by selecting them and dragging to the desired position. To copy an object, position the mouse pointer on or inside the object, hold <Shift> and drag the mouse to the desired position.

To size an object, position the mouse pointer on a black handle and then drag the handle until the object is the desired shape and size. If you size a text object, Ami Pro changes the point size of the text automatically.

To delete an object, select the object and press <Del>. To delete a drawing double-click the frame to access 'Draw' mode, click the 'Select All' command icon and press <Del>.

It is time now to try some of these commands out. Save the document we used to open the frames as FRAME1.SAM, for safe keeping.

Double click in the picture frame, to activate the 'Draw' mode and click the 'Text' icon. Change the Font to Arial 18 with the **Text**, **Font** command and type 'Mouse' anywhere in the frame. Now click first on the 'Selection Arrow' icon and then on the newly created word, or text object. You should see a set of handles appear. Drag the text onto the body of the mouse and rotate it in line with the rest of the drawing by selecting **Draw**, **Rotate** and completing the dialogue box as shown here.

Now, while the text is still selected, you can change any of its format properties in the **Text** sub-menu, so try making it red. As a final contribution to modern art, let us try some free hand sketching. Select 'Polyline', hold down the <Shift> key and draw a freehand mouse (animal type!) below the text. This

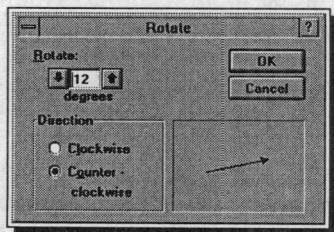

might end up as several different objects, but we hope your artistry is better than ours, shown below.

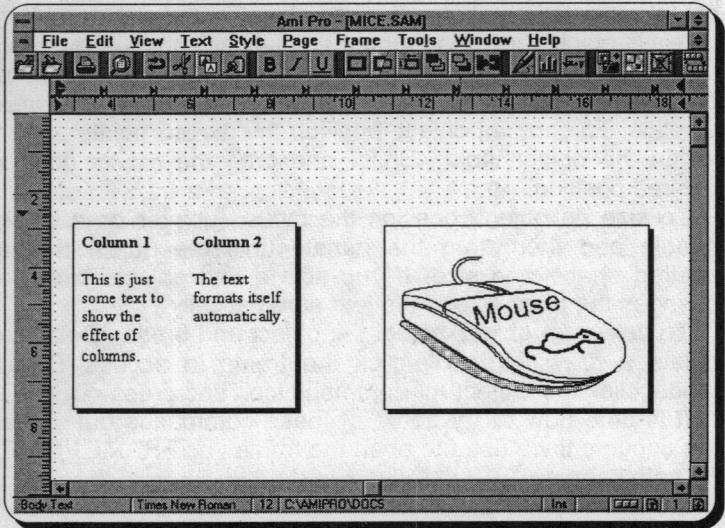

Grouping Objects:

You now have several objects in the picture frame, which, if you are not careful, will all move independently during editing and spoil the effect. We need to group them together. When you group objects, Ami Pro treats them as one unit. You can use the 'Group' toggle command icon or choose **Draw**, **Group** to do this. You can then move, copy, size, delete, and use any of the 'Draw' commands on the group of objects and they will all stay together.

To group our objects select the first one, hold <Shift> and click the next object. Repeat for each object you want to include in the group and then click the 'Group' command icon. A quicker way, as we want to group all the objects, would be to click the 'Select All' icon. Ami Pro displays black handles around the group of objects instead of around each individual one.

Using Layered Objects:

You can use the 'Bring to Front' and 'Send to Back' command icons or choose **Draw**, **Bring to Front** or **Send to Back** to determine the order of layered objects. Objects layered on top of each other can create useful visual effects.

In some ways Ami Pro treats objects within a frame in very much the same way as it treats frames itself, the procedures for grouping and layering frames being the same as those for grouping and layering objects. With frames, layering is a useful method to overcome the fact that you cannot place a graphic in a text frame; you simply layer a transparent text frame on top of the picture frame. When both are satisfactory you should then 'Group' the frames together, to keep them intact.

Using Fill Patterns:

You can use the 'Fill Pattern' icon to specify a colour and fill pattern for selected closed objects such as polygons, squares, and circles. The first time you access 'Draw' mode, the fill pattern is transparent. Ami Pro uses the pattern and colour you specify for both currently selected objects and any future objects you draw.

Using a Grid:

A grid is used to align objects in the drawing. The 'Grid' command is a toggle, you can switch it on or off. To align objects on the grid use the 'Snap To' command icon, this works whether or not the grid is displayed in the frame.

Saving a Drawing as a Graphic File:

You can save a drawing, or an object in a drawing, as an AmiDraw file, a Windows Metafile, or a Windows Bitmap file. You can then use your best drawings as clip art at some time in the future.

To save a drawing as a graphic file, select the frame that contains it, choose **Tools**, **Drawing** and **File**, **Save As Drawing** and complete the dialogue box produced.

We leave it to you to decide whether it is worth saving your mice for posterity.

9. MANAGING DOCUMENTS

Document Checking

When you have entered all the text and graphics into your document and selected suitable formats, there is only the process of correcting your work before printing the final copy. Ami Pro has many built-in tools to speed this process up and we will briefly describe the main ones here. There is also a set of SmartIcons for document checking and correcting.

Using the Spell Checker:

Most people have trouble spelling at least some words, but with Ami Pro that is not a problem. The package has a very comprehensive spell checker with two dictionaries. The main dictionary contains some 115,000 words which cannot be edited. The other is a user dictionary that you can customise and edit. When you use Spell Check and choose Add To Dictionary, Ami Pro adds the word to the user dictionary, which has the file name LTSUSER1.DIC and is stored by default in the \LOTUSAPP\SPELL directory.

To spell check your document, either click the 'Spell check' SmartIcon, or select **Tools**, **Spell Check** to open the dialogue box which is shown alongside. Unless you moved the cursor to the front of the document, select the **Check from beginning of document** button. The 'other text streams' referred to includes text in frames, etc.

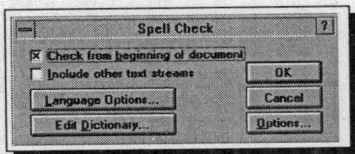

The first time you use the Spell checker you should select **Language Options** in the second box shown. As you can see the default in the UK is a choice between British, British IZE and American. In this country, you would normally select British in the two windows the first time you open it and never need to touch it

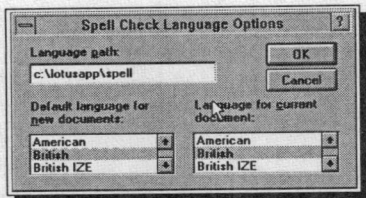

again. You should note, however, that there are several other languages available, if you ever need them.

If you select **Options** from the opening box you can turn on, or off, the four options shown alongside. The last one is the only one that needs comment. You would normally select this to **Include user dictionary alternatives** in the list of alternatives Ami Pro offers to replace a misspelled, or unrecognised, word. If you leave this blank you will not be offered your own dictionary contents in the box below.

When you have selected the options you want, select **OK** to start the Spell Checking operation. When the program encounters a word not in either dictionary it will highlight the word in the document text, so that you can see the context, and the following box will open.

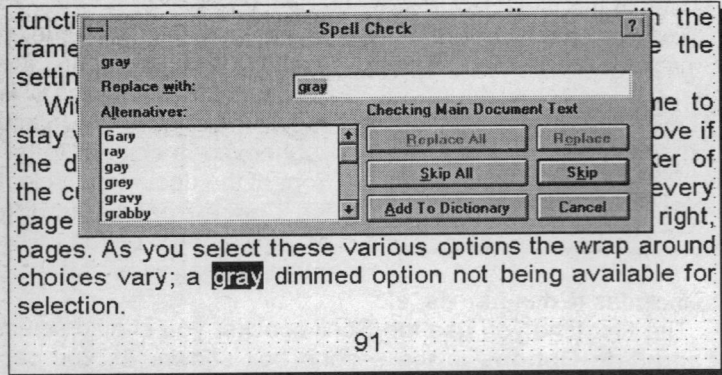

The problem word, in this case 'gray', is placed in the top left corner of the box (in case you forget it) and is selected in the **Replace with** window. If you agree that the spelling is incorrect, you have the options of clicking on one of the **Alternatives** in the presented list, or of manually editing the highlighted word in the window. You would then select

106

Replace, to change only the current error, or **Replace All** to change every occurrence of 'gray' in the document.

Once you have changed the **Replace with** window you are given the extra options of **Skip**ping one, or all occurrences in the document, or of saving the alteration to your dictionary.

If you selected the **Check for repeated words** option, the box shown here is opened whenever two adjacent words are found in the document. You are then placed in the previous box to take whatever action you think best.

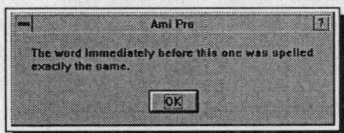

Ami Pro's Spell Checker is very powerful and well worth using, but you do sometimes need a little patience and the alternatives offered can sometimes be quite amusing.

Using the Thesaurus:

Another vast improvement over previous versions of Ami Pro, is the thesaurus. In its present form it is indispensable. Apparently it holds 'over 1,400,000 words to help it find definitions, variations, and synonyms for 40,000 root words'. To use the thesaurus simply place the cursor on the word you want to look up and select **Tools, Thesaurus**. As long as the word is recognised the following box will open.

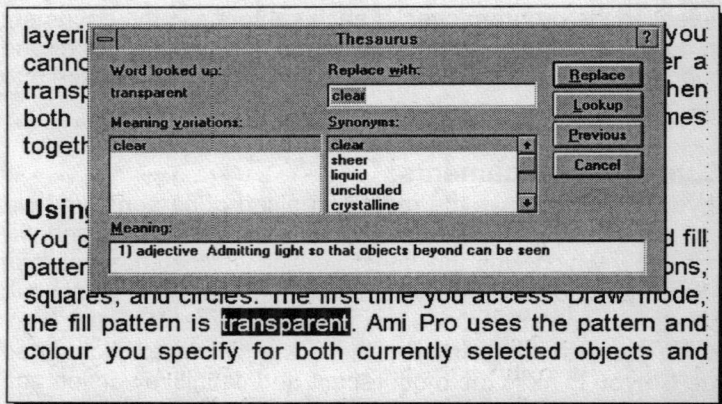

layeri... you
canno... er a
trans... hen
both ... mes
togeth...

Usin...
You c... d fill
patter... ons,
squares, and circles. The first time you access Draw mode, the fill pattern is transparent. Ami Pro uses the pattern and colour you specify for both currently selected objects and

107

This is a very powerful tool. If you want to see information about an item in the **Meaning variations** list, such as its **Meaning**, then select it. To change the word in the **Replace with** text box, select a different word in either the **Meaning variations** or **Synonyms** list box, or type a word directly into the text box.

You can use the thesaurus like a simple dictionary by typing any word into the **Replace with** box and selecting **Look up**. If the word is recognised, its meaning, and lists of variations and synonyms will be displayed. Pressing <Enter> will place the word into the document.

The Grammar Checker:
The grammar checker provided with Ami Pro, we feel falls in a different league. The idea is excellent, but whenever we have tried to use it we have given up in exasperation. If you select **Tools**, **Grammar Check** the following box is opened. You have the choice of seven types of writing styles, namely casual, formal, academic, fiction, technical, legal and business. When you have made your selection the program checks each sentence in the document in turn and offers comments about the writing style and suggestions of possible improvements. In our experience one suggestion in four was usable.

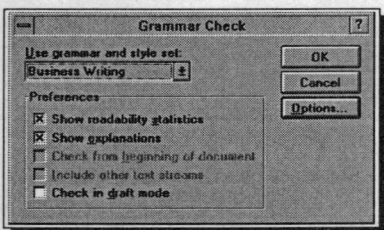

Comparing Documents:
If you are not always the most organised of persons, you will at time end up with several files with similar names and will not know which was the latest version. Sometimes you can simply look for the one with the latest date and delete the others - or can you? Does this scenario sound familiar? If so, when you are using Ami Pro there is a simple solution. Load the file you think is the most recent and definitive version and select **Doc Compare** from the **Tools** menu.

108

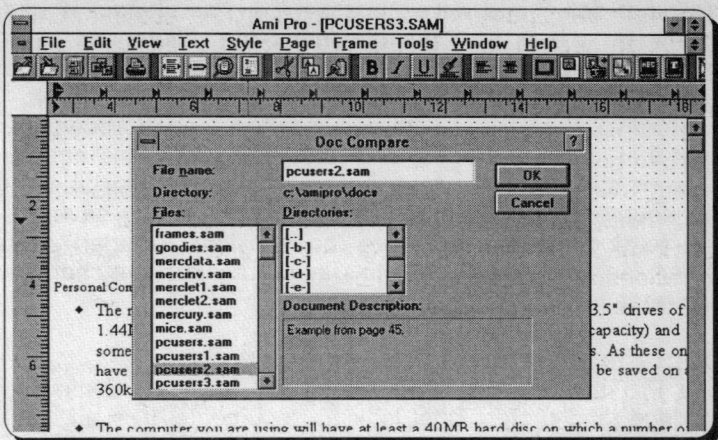

```
┌──────────────────────────────────────────────────────────┐
│ ═  Ami Pro - [PCUSERS3.SAM]                          ▼ ◆   │
├──────────────────────────────────────────────────────────┤
│  File  Edit  View  Text  Style  Page  Frame  Tools  Window  Help │
└──────────────────────────────────────────────────────────┘
```

Doc Compare dialog:

File name: pcusers2.sam
Directory: c:\amipro\docs
Files:
frames.sam
goodies.sam
mercdata.sam
mercinv.sam
merclet1.sam
merclet2.sam
mercury.sam
mice.sam
pcusers.sam
pcusers1.sam
pcusers2.sam
pcusers3.sam

Directories:
[..]
[-b-]
[-c-]
[-d-]
[-e-]

Document Description:
Example from page 45.

OK   Cancel

Personal Com...
* The r... 3.5" drives of
  1.44I... capacity) and
  some... s. As these on
  have... be saved on
  360k...

* The computer you are using will have at least a 40MB hard disc on which a number o...

Your screen might look something like that above. In this example we wanted to check the differences between PCUSERS3, which was loaded, and PCUSERS2, which is highlighted in the **Files** window. As soon as we selected PCUSERS2 its name was placed in the **File name** window.

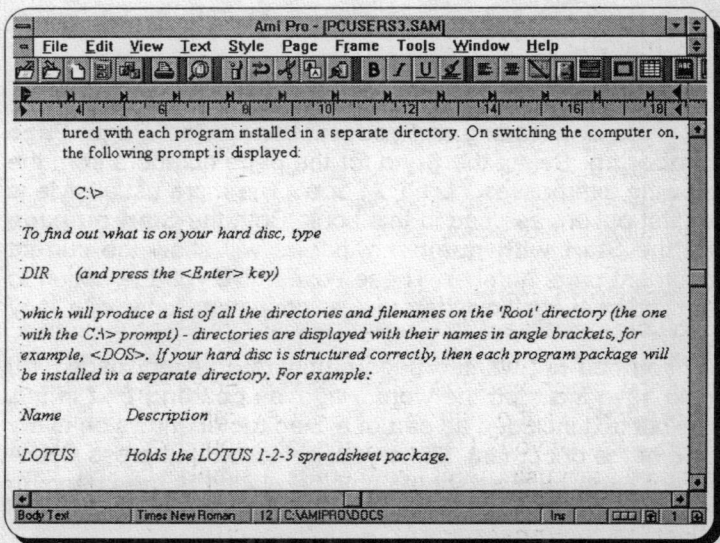

tured with each program installed in a separate directory. On switching the computer on, the following prompt is displayed:

C:\>

To find out what is on your hard disc, type

DIR   (and press the <Enter> key)

which will produce a list of all the directories and filenames on the 'Root' directory (the one with the C:\> prompt) - directories are displayed with their names in angle brackets, for example, <DOS>. If your hard disc is structured correctly, then each program package will be installed in a separate directory. For example:

Name   Description

LOTUS   Holds the LOTUS 1-2-3 spreadsheet package.

No other selections were necessary; on selecting **OK** and moving to the end of the document the differences were immediately and colourfully shown as can be seen at the bottom of the previous page.

Ami Pro shows any differences in the loaded document. Text that is in the loaded, or source document, and not the other, is shown in blue italic. Text that is in the other and not the source is shown in red strike-through. If you save the source document it will have the revisions included in it. Otherwise, use **File, Revert to Saved** to cancel the changes and retrieve the document as it was.

Document Referencing

Ami Pro has always been strong on features needed to produce long professional looking documents. It is an ideal medium for working with books, theses and other technical papers.

Page Numbering:

If your document needs numbered pages, it is very easy to do. Decide where on the page you want the number to be placed and put the cursor there. In the example shown on the facing page the selected location is centred, in the bottom page margin.

As long as you are in 'Layout' mode, you can place the cursor in the bottom margin and press <Ctrl+E> to achieve this. Type any leading text you want and select **Page, Page Numbering**. Select the **Style** for the page numbers from the following alternatives, '1, I, i, A, or a'. The more usual style is the first option, as used in this book. Both the **Start on page** and the **Start with number** windows will show the current document page number. These boxes give you the option to start numbering anywhere in a document and with any number.

If you had not wanted page numbers on every page, you could have included the word 'Page' as **Leading text** in this box, but text included as part of a fixed footer shows on every page of the document. Make your selection and press **OK**. A correct page number should now be placed at the bottom of all the selected pages in the document, no matter on which page you actually entered the information.

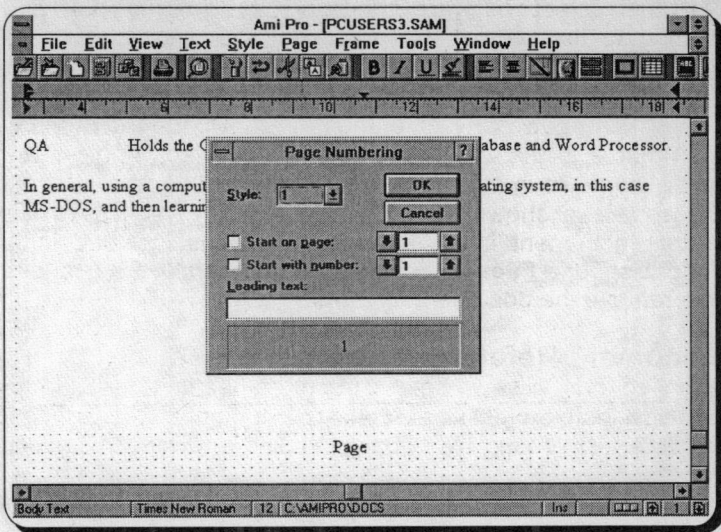

Using Footnotes:

If your document requires footnotes at the end of each page, or endnotes at the end of each chapter, they are very easy to add and later, if necessary, to edit. Place the cursor at the position you want the reference point to be in the document and select **Tools**, **Footnotes**. A dialogue box is opened as shown in the screen simulation on the next page.

This shows both the box and the results obtained by actioning it, both on the same page. The first reference point was placed after the word 'Basic' on the top line. The default options in the dialogue box were accepted, Ami Pro then placed the line across the bottom of the page, the reference number against the left margin and indented the cursor position ready for us to type in the reference information - a very painless operation.

Select **Options** if you want endnotes at the end of your document, (instead of footnotes at the end of each page), a different numbering system, or to customise the line and indenting of the text. You can edit the text, delete, or add more references whenever you want and Ami Pro will take care of the numbering for you.

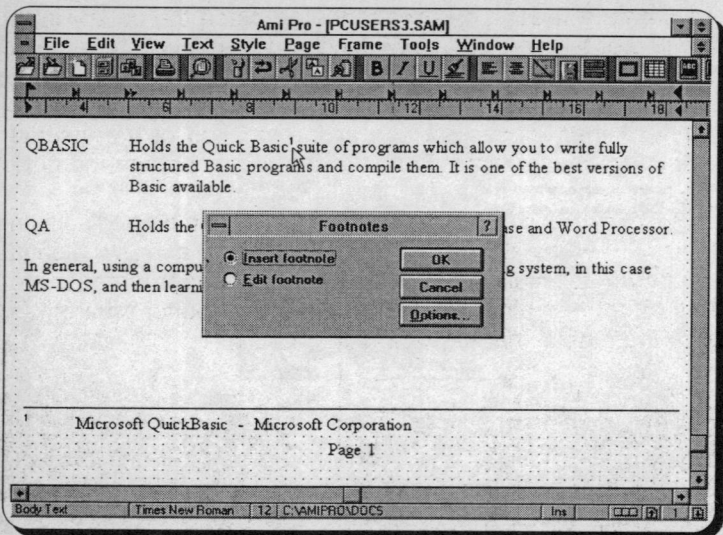

Using Headers and Footers:

Headers consist of text placed in the top margin area of a page, whereas footers are text in the bottom margin. There are two types of headers and footers in Ami Pro.

Fixed ones, that are produced in the same position of every page in a document; and floating ones that only appear after they are placed.

We used a fixed footer to place page numbering earlier in the chapter. When in 'Layout' mode you place fixed headers and footers in exactly the same way; simply type the text you want into the upper, or lower, margin areas of any page in the document. You can format the text in all the usual ways and use styles with it. The header and footer area layout controls, such as margins, number of lines and tabs, etc., are accessed with the **Page**, **Modify Page Layout** commands covered in an earlier chapter.

If you want multiple headers or footers in the same document, you can insert floating headers or footers. Ami repeats the header or footer text until it encounters either another floating header or footer, or an inserted page layout, in the document.

To create a floating header or footer, place the cursor in the top line of the first page on which you want it to show, select **Page**, **Header/Footer**, click on the **Floating Header/Footer** button and make the selections you want, in the opened box. Ami Pro then places a mark at the location of the insertion point. Type your required text in the top or bottom margin of the first page.

You can stop floating header/footer text from displaying later in your document, by inserting a new floating header/footer mark where you want the header/footer to stop and then not typing any text in the top or bottom margin, so creating a blank header or footer.

Outline Mode

Outline mode provides a way for you to view and organise the contents of a document. Nine outline levels can be used and these are based upon the paragraph styles of your document. Each type of heading paragraph style has an outline level assigned to it.

Assigning Outline Levels:

'Outline' levels are stored as part of the formatting information in the paragraph styles, so you must assign these levels to your paragraph styles before you can usefully use 'Outline' mode. Then your outline will automatically display your document headings at the correct levels. This is an easy process carried out by selecting the **Style**, **Outline Style** command to open the dialogue box shown on the next page.

Initially a list of all your document styles will display in the right hand window column under the 'None' heading. This means that none of them have been given an 'Outline style' level yet. You rank your heading styles, as shown, with the highest ranking style in the '1' position. The easiest way to do this is to drag the style name across the window and release it under the correct column heading.

You can also do this without a mouse using the **Promote** and **Demote** buttons of the dialogue box.

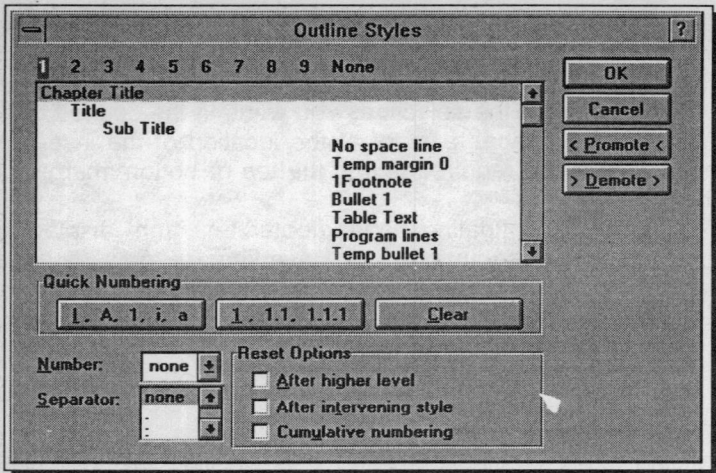

Outline Numbering:

The remainder of the box is devoted to the selection of paragraph numbering schemes. If you want all your paragraphs numbered, you must rank all the styles and then assign one of the numbering schemes. The easiest way is by clicking the left **Quick Numbering** button. The numbering scheme selected will then be shown in the ranking window above. If not quite correct, you can customise it, by highlighting a style in the list and making selections from the **Number** and **Separator** windows. You are even given the option of including brackets in the numbers.

If you want a ready made document to examine in this mode, load the file README31.SAM, which should be in your \Amipro\Docs directory. Then select **View**, **Outline Mode,** or click on the 'Toggle outline/layout view' SmartIcon. The screen on the next page shows the document in 'Outline' mode.

This document is well worth reading as it contains details of all the updates included in version 3.1 of Ami Pro. Most of these are not mentioned anywhere else.

When you access 'Outline' mode, outline 'level' and 'command' icons are displayed across the top of the screen,

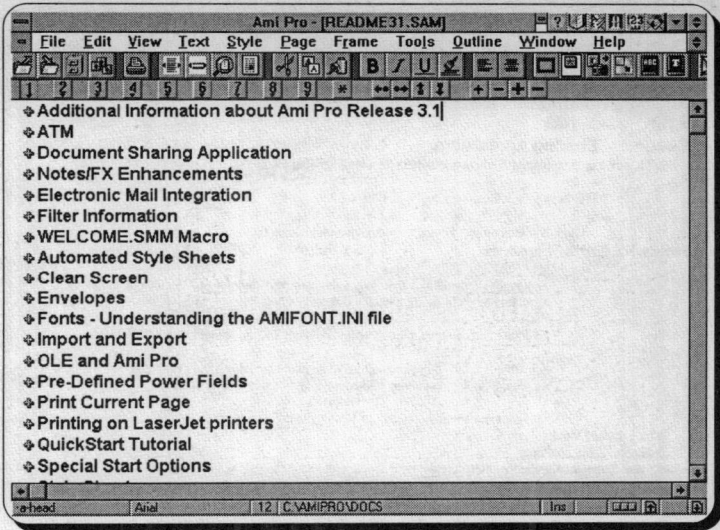

```
                    Ami Pro - [README31.SAM]
 -  File  Edit  View  Text  Style  Page  Frame  Tools  Outline  Window  Help
```

◇ Additional Information about Ami Pro Release 3.1|
◇ ATM
◇ Document Sharing Application
◇ Notes/FX Enhancements
◇ Electronic Mail Integration
◇ Filter Information
◇ WELCOME.SMM Macro
◇ Automated Style Sheets
◇ Clean Screen
◇ Envelopes
◇ Fonts - Understanding the AMIFONT.INI file
◇ Import and Export
◇ OLE and Ami Pro
◇ Pre-Defined Power Fields
◇ Print Current Page
◇ Printing on LaserJet printers
◇ QuickStart Tutorial
◇ Special Start Options

as shown. The level buttons are numbered from '1' to '9', followed by an 'asterisk'. The screen view above shows when the '1' level button has been pressed.

Outline Level Icons:

You click the desired outline level button, or icon, to display all the document text using the paragraph style set to that outline level, plus any text using paragraph styles set to higher outline levels.

If you have README31.SAM open, click on the second level button to see the second ranked headings display on the screen. Clicking the '*' icon opens up all the text in the document.

Experiment with these buttons to open and close the document, another part of which is shown on the next page, with more detail opened. This view can be obtained if the '5' level button is clicked, (or any of the buttons from '6' to '9', as they do not have Outline styles attached to them).

115

File   Edit   View   Text   Style   Page   Frame   Tools   Outline   Window   Help

⬦ **Additional Information about Ami Pro Release 3.1**
⬦ **ATM**
⬦ **Document Sharing Application**
  ⬦ **To access Document Sharing information in Ami Pro Help**
     1.
     Choose Help/Contents.
   ⬦ 2.
     Click the Document Sharing icon.
⬦ **Notes/FX Enhancements**
     •
     The eight user-defined Doc Info fields are now defined per document as
     opposed to eight fields globally defined in Ami Pro,
     •
     FX fields can now be placed within an Ami Pro document more than once,
     •
     Ami Pro 3.1 has been fine tuned to exploit the advantages cf Notes/FX 1.1,
     including faster launching and more efficient document handling,
   ⬦ •
     Three new implementations of Notes Field Exchange.
  ⬦ **Doc-Level Variables**
  ⬦ **Macro field passing**
  ⬦ **Five Custom Fields**

e-head   Arial   12   C:\AMIPRO\DOCS   Ins

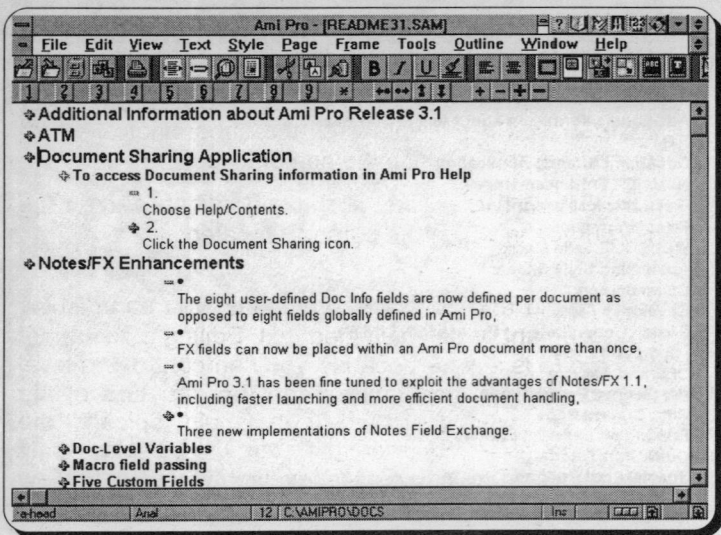

Outline Command Icons:

To use the command buttons explained below place the
cursor in the paragraph you want to manipulate and click the
desired outline command icon. Several of the commands
available as icons are also available under the **Outline**
menu, which is only available when you are in 'Outline' mode.

PROMOTE - Assigns a paragraph to a higher outline
and paragraph level.

DEMOTE - Assigns a paragraph to a lower outline
and paragraph level.

MOVE UP - Moves selected text to the position before
the paragraph preceding it.

MOVE DOWN - Moves selected text to the position
after the paragraph following it.

SMALL PLUS - Displays any hidden subordinate text
for the paragraph in which the cursor is located, one
outline level at a time.

116

SMALL MINUS - Hides any displayed subordinate text for the paragraph in which the cursor is located, one outline level at a time.

LARGE PLUS - Displays all the subordinate text for the paragraph in which the cursor is located.

LARGE MINUS - Hides all the subordinate text for the paragraph in which the cursor is located.

Using the expand and contract commands, you can display the entire document or only selected text. Editing a document in 'Outline' mode is simple because you can control the level of detail that displays and quickly see the structure of the document. If you want to focus on the main topics in the document, you can contract the text to display only paragraph styles set to high outline levels. If you want to view additional detail, you can expand the text to display text using paragraph styles set to lower outline levels.

Outline Buttons:
Another feature of the 'Outline' mode is the buttons placed before each paragraph. These not only show the status of the paragraph, but can be used to quickly manipulate paragraph text. If you want to hide these outline buttons, deselect **Outline buttons** in the **View**, **View Preferences** dialogue box.

PLUS BUTTON - Indicates that the paragraph is using a paragraph style set to an outline level between 1 and 9 and that the paragraph has subordinate text.

MINUS BUTTON - Indicates that the paragraph is using a paragraph style set to an outline level between 1 and 9 and that the paragraph does not have any subordinate text.

FILLED PLUS BUTTON - Indicates that the paragraph is using a paragraph style set to an outline level between 1 and 9 and that the paragraph has subordinate text that is currently hidden.

BOX BUTTON - Indicates that the paragraph is using a paragraph style set to an outline level of None. Ami Pro displays this text halfway between two outline level icons.

To display, or hide, subordinate text double-click a 'Plus' button. Click on a 'Plus' button and drag it, to move text to a new location. Ami Pro automatically moves the text as you drag the mouse.

If you print from 'Outline' mode only the text that is exposed on the screen will actually print. Subordinate text and the outline buttons do not print.

10. MORE ADVANCED TECHNIQUES

TABLES

The ability to use 'Tables' is built into most top-range word processors these days. At first glance the process looks complicated and we are sure only a small percentage of users take advantage of the facility, which is a pity because using a 'Table' has many possibilities. They are used to create adjacent columns of text and numeric data. In Ami Pro you can use the 'Tables' feature in Layout, Draft, and Outline modes and you can include pictures, charts, notes, footnotes, tabs, and page breaks in your tables. There are several ways to place information into a table:

- Type the desired text, or numeric data.
- Paste text from the main document.
- Paste link information from another Windows application.
- Insert data created in another application.
- Import a picture.
- Create a drawing, chart or equation.

The data is placed into individual cells that are organised into columns and rows, similar to a spread sheet. You can modify the appearance of table data by applying text formatting and enhancements, or by using different paragraph styles.

Creating a Table:

Tables can be of two types, either placed directly onto a document page, or placed within a frame. If you know your table will be larger than one page, you should create a page table, otherwise place it in a frame. Ami Pro automatically continues a page table onto subsequent pages.

As an example we will step through the process of creating the table shown on the next page, which was created in a frame, using the '_default.sty' style. Open a frame, as shown, across the full width of the page and about one screen high. Select the frame by clicking in it and choose **Tools**, **Tables**, or click on the 'Create a table' SmartIcon. Select 5 columns and 13 rows and the default **Layout** options shown in the lower dialogue box on the next page. These will be altered later, as necessary.

ADEPT CONSULTANTS - QUARTERLY ANALYSIS				
	JANUARY	FEBRUARY	MARCH	TOTALS
INCOME:				
Consulting	12,000.00	13,500.00	14,250.00	39,750.00
TOTAL	12,000.00	13,500.00	14,250.00	39,750.00
COSTS:				
Salaries	3,000.00	3,600.00	4,000.00	10,600.00
Travel expenses	1,200.00	1,800.00	1,450.00	4,450.00
Rent	500.00	500.00	500.00	1,500.00
Electricity	850.00	825.00	675.00	2,350.00
Phone/fax	800.00	925.00	750.00	2,475.00
TOTAL	6,350.00	7,650.00	7,375.00	21,375.00
Operating Profit	5,650.00	5,850.00	6,875.00	18,375.00

When you select **OK** a table of cells will display, with the cursor placed in the top left cell. To access a page table from the main document, you click anywhere in the table. To access a frame table, like the one we are working with, you

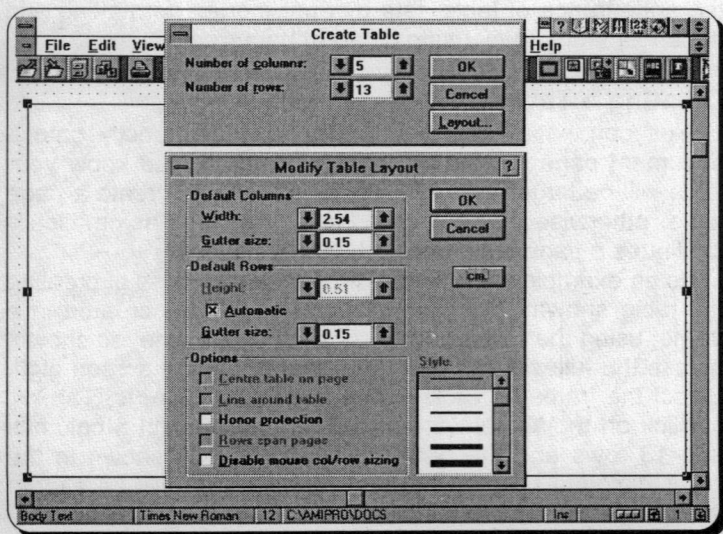

double-click inside the frame. To move around in a table, simply click the desired cell, and to exit a table, click anywhere outside it.

Move the cursor into the second row, either with the mouse, or one of the following keyboard commands, and type the headings as shown on the next page.

Navigating with the Keyboard :

To access a page table with the keyboard, place the cursor on the line above the table and press the down arrow, '↓'. To access a frame table, select the desired frame using **Go To**.

Press this	*To do this*
Tab	Moves the cursor from left to right, cell by cell in a row.
Shift+Tab	Moves the cursor, as above, but from right to left (in the opposite direction).
Ctrl+↑	Moves the cursor up one row.
Ctrl+↓	Moves the cursor down one row.
Ctrl+→	Moves the cursor right one column.
Ctrl+←	Moves the cursor left one column.
Home	Moves the cursor to the beginning of the current line within a cell.
Home, Home	Moves the cursor to the first column in the current row.
End	Moves the cursor to the end of the current line within a cell.
End, End	Moves the cursor to the last column in the current row.
↑,↓,←, and →	Moves the cursor within cells, between cells, and between the cells in a page table and the main document text.

To exit a page table and return to the main document text, press <Esc>; to exit a frame table, press <Esc> twice.

Entering Text:

As you enter the heading text in your table it will, by default, left-align in the cell. Look at the 'Style Status' button and you should see a new style name there, namely, '·Table Text'.

When you create a table, Ami Pro generates a 'Table Text' paragraph style, based upon the 'Body Text' style, except paragraph spacings and indents are set to zero, and there are no tabs or special effects. It assigns this paragraph style to all cells in the table. You can modify the style, or assign a different one to any cell in the table.

When you have entered all the headings on row 2, drag the pointer across them all, to select them and click on the 'Centre text' SmartIcon to centre-justify them. Now type in the left column headings. You will find that the column is not wide enough for some of them. But notice what happens in this case, Ami Pro adds a new line to *all the cells* in that row. This is one of the most useful aspect of 'Tables', in that you do not have to worry about the height of cells; they sort themselves out automatically.

You can use a mouse to modify column and row sizes if **Disable mouse col/row sizing** is not selected in the 'Modify Table Layout' dialogue box. Ami Pro does not allow you to increase the size of a column if the table fills the entire page. In which case you must decrease the size of another column first. With the mouse, drag the right boundary of row 1 to the right to widen the column. The mouse pointer changes to a four-headed arrow, to enable you to do this. The other way of changing the column width is to select **Ta**ble, **Column/Row Size** with the pointer in the column you want to change. In our case a column width of 3.25cm would be ideal.

Connecting Cells:

In our example the main heading takes up the whole of the top row and uses only one cell. You can connect two or more adjacent cells to create one large cell, by first selecting all the cells and choosing the **Ta**ble, **Connect Cells** command. If you later want to disconnect the cells, place the cursor in the connected cell and choose **Ta**ble, **Disconnect Cells**.

With the mouse there is a quick way to select a whole row, or column. Position the mouse pointer at the top of the column, or to the left of the desired row. The mouse pointer changes to a solid arrow. Click this to select the entire column or row, or drag to select multiple columns or rows.

When you have connected the top row press <Ctrl+E>, to select centred text and type in the main heading.

Entering Numerical Data:

Now add the numerical data to the table, as described below. You must type in only bare numbers, so that Ami Pro can recognise that the cell is numeric. While the cursor is in the cell, only the number displays, Ami Pro right-aligns it when you move the cursor to the next cell. If you type a space, or comma, or you press <Enter> in a number cell, the program treats the cell as a text cell instead of a number cell.

To show decimal places in the table select **Style**, **Modify Style**, **Table Format**, to display the dialogue box shown overleaf.

This dialogue box controls how numbers will display in your table. As shown, select Fixed decimal in **Cell format** to always display, two decimal places. If you need to, you can also set the Negative and Currency formats here.

Quick Add:

Enter the 'Consulting revenue' figures for the period January to March in row 4 and place the cursor in the 'Totals' column of that row. We do not need to calculate this figure, Ami Pro will do it for us. Select **Table**, **Quick Add**, **Row** and the total is automatically added to the cursor cell.

As long as all the cells in a row, or column, are numerical this procedure works well, but if an included cell is text based

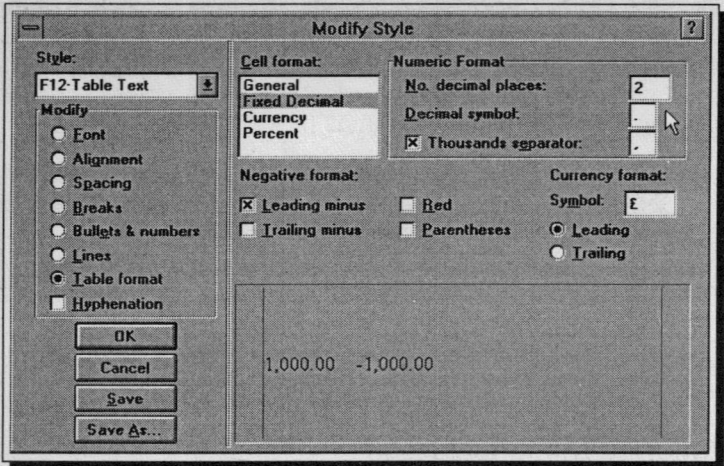

Modify Style dialog box showing:

Style: F12-Table Text

Modify:
- Font
- Alignment
- Spacing
- Breaks
- Bullets & numbers
- Lines
- Table format (selected)
- Hyphenation

[OK] [Cancel] [Save] [Save As...]

Cell format:
General
Fixed Decimal
Currency
Percent

Numeric Format:
No. decimal places: 2
Decimal symbol: .
[X] Thousands separator: ,

Negative format:
[X] Leading minus
[ ] Trailing minus
[ ] Red
[ ] Parentheses

Currency format:
Symbol: £
(•) Leading
( ) Trailing

1,000.00 -1,000.00

'Quick Add', or any formula referencing the cell, yields incorrect results, or displays the message 'REF' in the cell.

Manipulating Cell Data:

The figures in row 5 of our example are exactly the same as those in row 4, so you can copy them. To do this, select the row 4 cells with the mouse pointer and click on the 'Copy' SmartIcon. Move the cursor to the 'January Income Total' cell and press the 'Paste' SmartIcon. It's as easy as that to copy, or to move, data between cells. You could, of course, have used the **Edit**, **Copy** and **Paste** commands, but clicking on Icons is much faster. You can now practice entering more numerical data and complete the first 11 rows.

Using Formulas in Tables:

The last two rows of our table need formulas developed in them to calculate the results. 'Quick Add' cannot be used as it only operates on a whole row of figures.

Before we can develop even basic formulas we must have a way of referencing the cells. Ami Pro uses the Lotus 1-2-3 method of naming cells. Columns are named with letters, with 'A' being the first, starting from the left. Rows are named with numbers, with '1' being the top row. To make life easier if you are not familiar with spreadsheets, you can display column and row headings in the table. Choose **View, View Preferences** and select **Table row/column headings.**

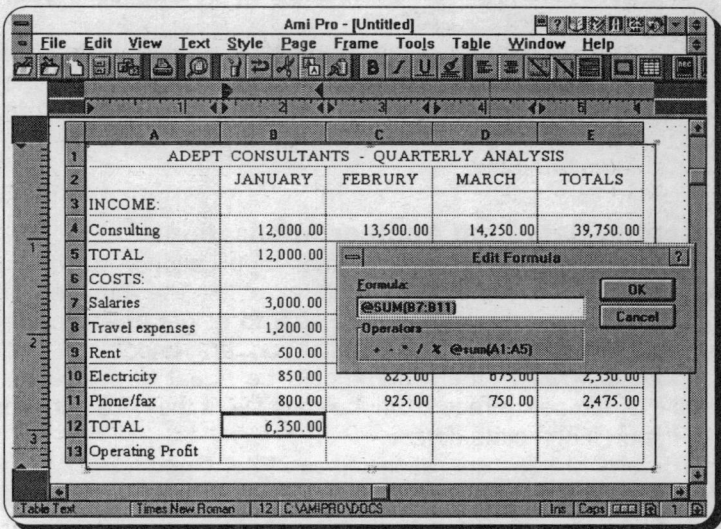

Place the cursor in cell B12, select **Table**, **Edit Formula** and enter the formula '@sum(b7:b11)' in the **Formula** window, to see a screen like that shown above.

You can use Lotus 1-2-3 syntax in table formulas, starting with an @, or an = or just use the operation. You can specify a range of cells using two periods (..) or a colon (:), as shown. When you place the insertion point in a cell that contains a formula, a box appears around the cell. The above menu command is used to edit existing formulas, as well as create them.

You can specify any combination of five mathematical operations in a formula. These are addition (+), subtraction (−), multiplication (*), division (/), and percent (%). Also, you can choose to sum a range of cells, as we have above, and you can nest operations within brackets.

Now copy the above '@ sum' formula to cells C12 and D12. The formula to put in cell B13, to calculate the

'Operating profit' for the month is (B5–B12). Simply copy this formula to cells C13 and D13 and you have completed the table. It should now look very similar to that at the beginning of the section. If you have not done so already save your document as TABLE2.SAM

The main reason for using formulas in a table, instead of just typing in the numbers, is that formulas will still give the correct final answer even if some of the data is changed. In this case you simply correct the data cells and Ami Pro recalculates the table.

Inserting Data from Another Application:

You can import data from other applications, such as spreadsheets or databases, into a table. The number of columns in the table should be equal to or greater than the number of fields in the data file you are importing. The number of rows in the table should be equal to or greater than the number of records in the data file. If they are not you will import incomplete data.

To carry out this operation choose **File**, **Open**, specify the data file format and name, and then select **Insert**, instead of the usual **OK**. Ami Pro inserts the text starting in the column in which the cursor was located, but only imports the amount of data that fits into the existing cells in the table. If you are importing a spreadsheet, Ami Pro displays a message asking you for the amount of data you want to insert.

Creating a Heading:

If a page table continues on multiple pages, you can create a table heading, which displays as the first row on each page, above the data rows.

To create a heading place the cursor in the top row of the first page of the table and choose the toggle command **Table**, **Headings**. You can change the heading on other pages by placing the cursor in a different row and making another selection

Using Table Data in a Chart:

If you want to generate a chart (graph) from your table data, simply select the data cells you want to process and **Copy** them to the Windows Clipboard; Ami Pro will use them when you create a chart, as described in the next section.

Charting Your Data

The 'Charting' function is used to create a variety of different graphs and charts. The process uses numeric data, separated by tabs or spaces, to create charts in an empty frame. There are two ways to input the data to the 'Charting' function:

a) To cut, or copy, the data from your main document text, or a table in an Ami Pro document, or from another application, to the Windows Clipboard.

b) To type the data directly into the Charting Data dialogue box.

In the last section you should have created a table of data which is ideal to demonstrate how Ami Pro charts are created. Load the previously saved file TABLE2.SAM. If you did not produce it you can simply enter the data into the 'Charting' function, or better still, go back and work your way through the section on 'Tables'.

As it stands the table data is not contiguous and is unsuitable for our purpose, so delete rows 3, 4, 5, 6 and 13, to produce a simplified 'Costs' data table as shown on the next page.

We will prepare a bar graph to compare the cost items over the first three-month period. Highlight the area shown on the next page and select **Edit**, **Copy** to place the required data on the Windows clipboard. Now open a suitable frame in your document to receive the chart, and with this frame selected, choose **Tools**, **Charting.** If you have no data table simply select **Tools**, **Charting**, answer 'Yes' to the question regarding data entry and then type the data, as shown, into the 'Charting Data' box produced. The resulting screen, similar to that below, should be the same with both methods.

127

	A	B	C	D	E
1	ADEPT CONSULTANTS - QUARTERLY ANALYSIS				
2		JANUARY	FEBRUARY	MARCH	TOTALS
3	Salaries	3,000.00	3,600.00	4,000.00	10,600.00
4	Travel expenses	1,200.00	1,800.00	1,450.00	4,450.00
5	Rent	500.00	500.00	500.00	1,500.00
6	Electricity	850.00	825.00	675.00	2,350.00
7	Phone/fax	800.00	925.00	750.00	2,475.00
8	TOTAL	6,350.00	7,650.00	7,375.00	21,375.00

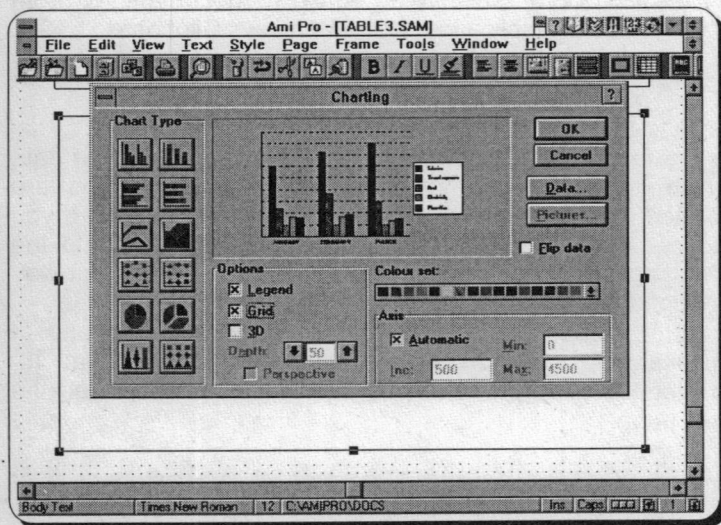

This 'Charting' dialogue box lets you make the final choices for your graph.

Our sample has selected a **Legend** to identify the columns. When this option is chosen the left titles column in the data input is used to generate the legend text. The **Grid** option displays dashed grid lines behind the chart. The lines align with the values on the axis of the chart, and may be horizontal or vertical, depending upon the type of chart. **3D** displays the chart with a multidimensional effect using the depth you specify. You can specify any number between 1 and 100. The **Perspective** option enhances the 3D effect in the chart.

Types of Chart:
The twelve coloured icons on the left of the previous dialogue box, are for selecting the different types of charts that Ami Pro can produce. How your data will look is shown in the middle 'Sample' window. In this case, a column chart is selected. Try clicking on the others and watch the results.

The chart types available (described from top to bottom) are normally used to show the following relationships between data:

Column	for comparing differences in data. Displays the values of dependent variables as two-dimensional vertical columns.
Stacked Column	for comparing cumulative data.
Bar	for comparing differences in data. Displays the values of dependent variables as two-dimensional horizontal bars.
Stacked Bar	for comparing cumulative data.
Line	for representing data values with points joined by lines and appearing at equal intervals along the x-axis. For such charts, the x-axis could be intervals in time, such as labels representing months.
Area Line	for representing the total in each category. A line chart in which the lines are stacked.
Line & Picture	These are X-Y charts. The data points need not appear in equal intervals along the x-axis.

Pie	for comparing parts with the whole. Displays data blocks as slices of a pie.
Exploded Pie	Same as a Pie but with slices 'exploded' from the pie.
Picture	Similar to a column chart, but each column is represented by a scaled picture. You can customise what pictures are displayed.
Stacked Picture	for comparing cumulative picture data.

When you have finished exploring and making entries in the 'Charting' box, select **OK** and watch Ami Pro automatically place your chart in the frame selected. It should look like the example shown below.

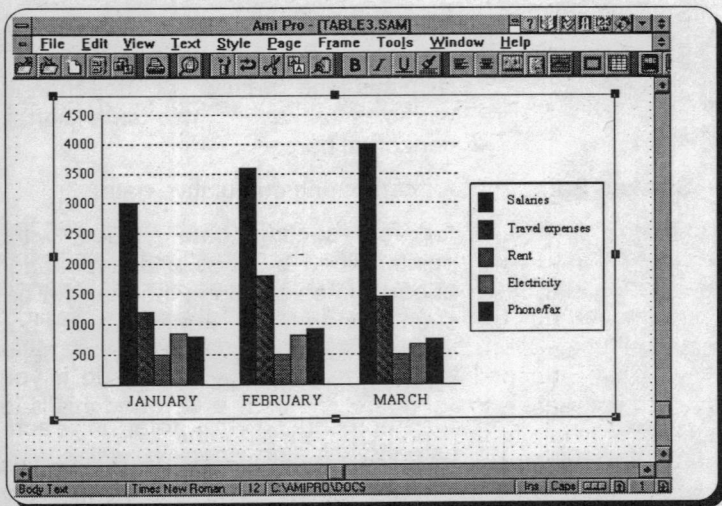

Improving an Ami Pro Chart:
An Ami Pro chart is in fact an AmiDraw file. Each value in the data used to create the chart, is a separate object within the chart. You can edit the chart by selecting **Tools**, **Drawing.**

130

You can then use any of the draw icons to move or modify selected objects, including text objects, or create new objects in the chart. In the example below, titles were added and the Legend object was modified.

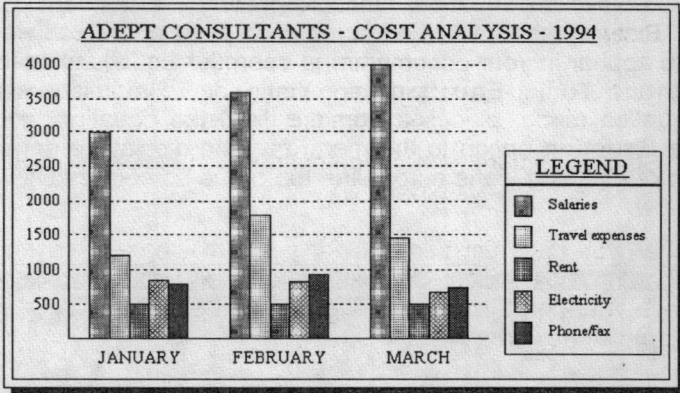

ADEPT CONSULTANTS - COST ANALYSIS - 1994

LEGEND
Salaries
Travel expenses
Rent
Electricity
Phone/Fax

JANUARY   FEBRUARY   MARCH

If you use Drawing to edit a chart, the next time you double-click on it Ami Pro changes to Draw mode. Ami Pro automatically chooses the last function you used on the chart.

Chart Frames:

One thing to remember with the 'Charting' feature is that the data you first used to create a chart is then linked, both to the chart and to the frame it is placed in. If you want to change this data you must do it with the **Data** option in the 'Charting' dialogue box. Even if you delete a chart the data for that chart stays attached to the frame, and will be used if you attempt to create another chart. The easy way round this is to delete the whole frame and then create another one.

We are sure that you will get many hours of fun with this feature and, more to the point, produce some very professional graphics for your report presentations.

Equations

Ami Pro includes one of the most powerful and intuitive Equations editor that we have seen. You can use it to create and edit scientific and mathematical formulae and equations and place them anywhere in your document.

To place an equation, function, or simply a mathematical or Greek symbol, position the insertion point where you want it to appear in your document and open the Equations editor, with the **Tools**, **Equations** command. Ami Pro changes to Equation mode, places a frame to hold the equation, adds the **Equation** option to the menu bar and displays a double set of equation icons across the top of the screen, as shown below.

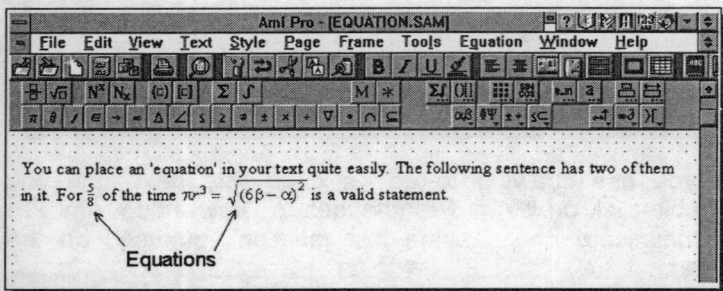

You simply build up the equation expression inside its frame with selections from the icons, or keystrokes. The frame, by default, flows with the document text and expands to include the equation. To leave Equation mode, click your mouse pointer outside the frame and to access Equation mode after you have created an equation, double-click inside the frame that contains the equation.

Equation Icons:

The icon bars contain six main sections as shown at the top of the next page. We do not intend, or indeed have the space, in this book to duplicate the program manual, so perhaps the easiest way to get a detailed description of these icons is to use the Ami Pro Help. This in fact covers the subject very well.

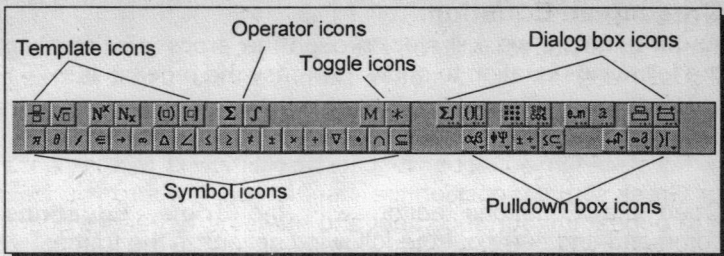

Template icons — Operator icons — Toggle icons — Dialog box icons — Symbol icons — Pulldown box icons

While in Equation mode, press the **F1** key and select the option **Using the Equation Template Icons** from the list displayed. This opens the screen shown below.

To see the icons themslves on this screen, as shown, simply click the 'hand' mouse pointer on the underlined green hypertext link **equation template icons**.

When you have worked out the different template icons and how they work, you can obtain detailed information on the other icon sets by moving through the next few Help screens with the **>>** button. In fact, if you want to master Equations, you should carry on in this way and read all the relevant Help screens.

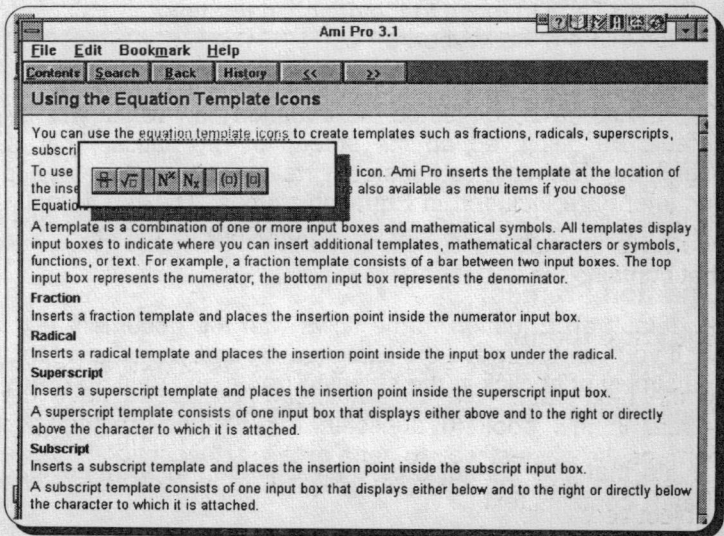

Ami Pro 3.1

File   Edit   Bookmark   Help

Contents | Search | Back | History | << | >>

Using the Equation Template Icons

You can use the equation template icons to create templates such as fractions, radicals, superscripts, subscri...

To use ... icon. Ami Pro inserts the template at the location of the inse... e also available as menu items if you choose Equatio...

A template is a combination of one or more input boxes and mathematical symbols. All templates display input boxes to indicate where you can insert additional templates, mathematical characters or symbols, functions, or text. For example, a fraction template consists of a bar between two input boxes. The top input box represents the numerator; the bottom input box represents the denominator.

Fraction
Inserts a fraction template and places the insertion point inside the numerator input box.

Radical
Inserts a radical template and places the insertion point inside the input box under the radical.

Superscript
Inserts a superscript template and places the insertion point inside the superscript input box.

A superscript template consists of one input box that displays either above and to the right or directly above the character to which it is attached.

Subscript
Inserts a subscript template and places the insertion point inside the subscript input box.

A subscript template consists of one input box that displays either below and to the right or directly below the character to which it is attached.

Creating an Equation:

As an example we will step through the process of creating the following equation to show how easy the process is.

$$\nabla^2 \sigma_p = \sqrt{\pi \frac{(1-\pi)}{n}}$$

Open the Equations editor, with the **Tools**, **Equations** command and carry out the following actions in the frame:

Click the ∇ Symbol icon
Click the Superscript Template icon
Type '2' followed by <Spacebar>, from the keyboard
Select σ from the Lowercase Greek Pulldown box
Click the Subscript Template icon
Type 'p' followed by <Spacebar>, from the keyboard
Type '=' from the keyboard to leave Subscript
Click the Radical Template icon to open the root sign
Click the π Symbol icon
Click the Fraction Template icon
Click the Parentheses Template icon
Type '1-' from the keyboard
Click the π Symbol icon
Press <Tab> to move to the denominator box
Type 'n' from the keyboard
Click outside the Equation frame to exit the editor.

You should have completed the equation now which will, by default, be displayed on the screen in red italics. This is useful so that you can instantly tell which parts of your document are included in Equation frames. The red actually prints the same as black text on a monochrome printer.

Equation Frames:

By default an Equation frame flows with the document text, but if you want to move the Equation around your document, you simply right click in the selected frame and select **Where Placed** in the Placement section of the Modify Frame Layout Box.

Note that you cannot create an Equation in a frame that already contains text.

11. FILE MANAGEMENT

The fact that Ami Pro documents are always linked to a style sheet, which is a separate file in its own right, adds a special importance to the file management function. You must take special precautions to ensure that the 'styles' files are available for your documents. This is no problem if all your work and printing is done from the same PC; but if you work on several different computers you will need to transport your files on floppy discs. The easy way to do this is with the Ami Pro File Management system, or with the macro which will be developed in the next chapter.

Listing Files:

To enter this linked program use the **File**, **File Management** command. The program box opened is shown in the example on page 74. All the files with a '*.S?M' name structure in the current directory are listed alphabetically, with their document description alongside.

To list other file types select **View**, which allows you to choose from the following: **All** to list all files in the directory, **Partial** to select a new file name template (for example, '*.sty' to list all the style files), or **Doc Info**, which produces a screen of information about the file which is highlighted on the list. You cannot edit anything on this information screen.

You select files from the list by clicking on their name with the mouse pointer. A further click will deselect them. Double clicking on a drive or directory name will open it.

Once selected you can move, copy, rename, delete and change the attributes of files by opening the **File** sub-menu. The example on the next page is a composite of the two dialogue boxes used during the **Copy** process.

The settings are to copy a file to a floppy disc in the A: drive, with the default being to **Take Associated Style Sheet**. If you accept this, a copy of the document's style sheet will be placed, with the file, at the designated destination. If your document uses any graphics files, for imported pictures, and these are not embedded in the file, you should check the **Take Associated Graphics Files** option.

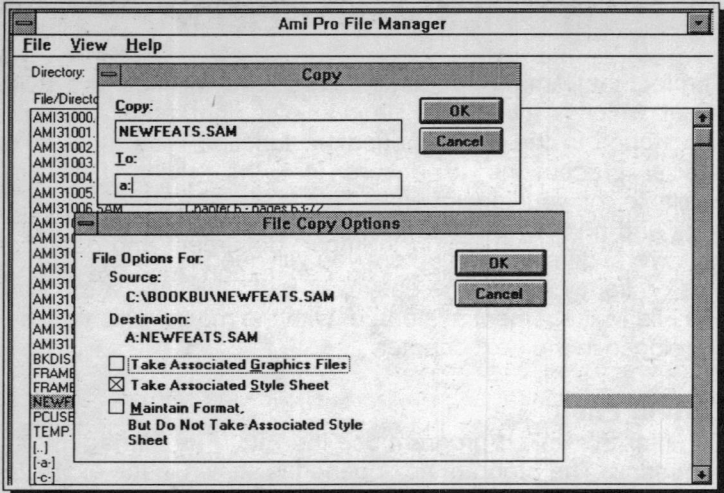

Ami Pro File Manager

File   View   Help

Directory:

Copy

Copy:
NEWFEATS.SAM

To:
a:

OK   Cancel

File Copy Options

File Options For:
   Source:
      C:\BOOKBU\NEWFEATS.SAM
   Destination:
      A:NEWFEATS.SAM

☐ Take Associated Graphics Files
☒ Take Associated Style Sheet
☐ Maintain Format,
   But Do Not Take Associated Style
   Sheet

OK   Cancel

If you select **Maintain Format** the paragraph styles and page layout information will be moved to the document, before it is copied. If you do not need to use the style sheet again, this is an easy way to simplify operations. If necessary, look back to the chapter on style sheets to remind yourself of the implications of styles embedded in the document.

The AMIFM Program:

The File Management program is held in a stand alone file called AMIFM.EXE, which is stored in the \AMIPRO directory, with all the other Ami Pro system files. To enable you to manipulate your Ami Pro files without having to load the whole program it is a good idea to copy this program into the same Windows group window as the Ami Pro icon.

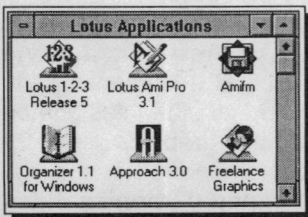

Lotus Applications

Lotus 1-2-3 Release 5   Lotus Ami Pro 3.1   Amifm

Organizer 1.1 for Windows   Approach 3.0   Freelance Graphics

To do this drag-copy the file from a Windows File Manager window and place it next to the Ami Pro icon. The icon symbol itself, as shown here, is moved as well and Windows looks after all the pathing information automatically.

To open the File Manager at any time you are in the Windows environment, simply double click its icon.

Importing and Exporting Data

To make Ami Pro an easy package for people to convert to, Lotus have provided a very extensive list of file conversion 'filters', which enable you to import document and data files made in other packages. You can export Ami Pro files to some of these packages as well.

File Formats Supported:

Ami Pro 3.1 claims to support the following formats, as listed in the manual and on the distribution disks. Both import and export filters are provided for those shown **emboldened** in the list. The remainder can be imported only. We have not tried out more than a handful of these!

1-2-3® releases 1, 1A, 2.0, and 2.01 (.WKS and .WK1)
1-2-3 releases 3.0, 3.1
1-2-3 for Windows (.WK3 and .WK4)
Advance Write
Ami Pro
ASCII
dBase III®, dBase III+®, and dBase IV®
DCA/FFT (Final Form Text)
DCA/RFT (Revisable Form Text)
DIF®
DisplayWrite® 4 and 5
E-Mail
Enable® versions 1-5 through 4.0
Executive MemoMaker
Lotus Manuscript® 2.0 and 2.1
Microsoft Excel version 5.0 and prior versions
Microsoft Word versions 4.0, 5.0, 5.1, and 5.5
MultiMate® version 3.3 and 4.0
MultiMate Advantage II
Navy DIF
Office Writer 6.2

Paradox® versions up to 3.5 (.DB)
Peach TextTM version 2.11 and prior versions
ProWrite versions 2.1 and 2.2
Q&A Write 1.x, 3.0 and 4.0
Rich Text Format
Samna® Word
SmartWare® version 1
SuperCalc® versions 3 and 4
Symphony® releases 1.x (.WRK and .WK1)
Wang (IWP) version 3.02
Windows Write
Word for Windows 6.0 and prior
WordPerfect versions 4.1 and 4.2
WordPerfect versions 5.0 and 5.1/5.2 and 6.0
WordStar® versions 3.3, 3.4, 4.1, and 5.0
WordStar 2000 versions 1.0 and 3.0
XYwrite III, III plus, IV and Windows

Ami Pro normally imports and exports the following formatting information, but only if the facility is available in the other package.

Alignment (centre, justify, left, right)
Capitalisation (initial caps, upper/ lower case, small caps)
Dates
Font (typeface, point size, colour)
Footnotes
Headers and footers
International characters
Line spacing
Page layout (margins, page breaks, rulers, tabs)
Page numbering
Paragraph styles
Special formatting (hard hyphens, non-breaking spaces)
Text frames
Text attributes (double underline, italic, bold, overstrike, strikethrough, superscript, subscript, underline, word underline)

Importing Files:

The importing operation is very straightforward and simply requires an extra entry in the dialogue box produced by the **File**, **Open** command.

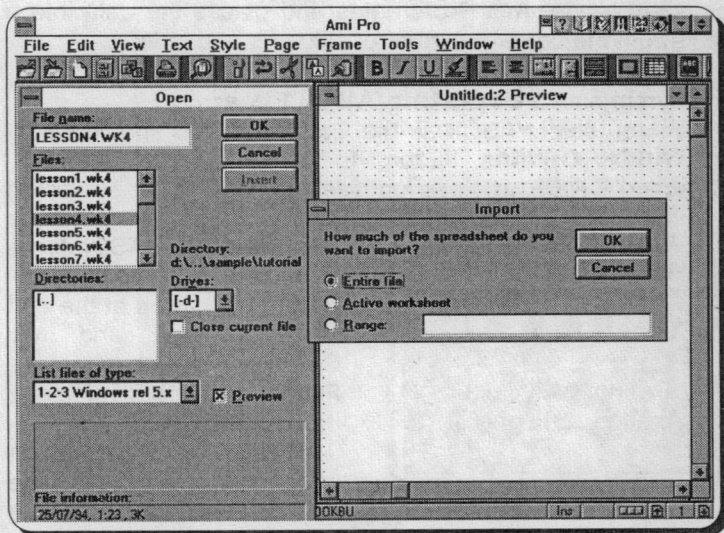

Select the type of file to import in the **List files of type** window. Where applicable Ami Pro places that application's default file extension in the **File name** window. '*.WK4' was used in the above example to search for Lotus 1-2-3 for Windows files. If the **Preview** option box is checked a preview window is opened on the right side of the screen, as above. In this case as a spreadsheet file has been selected a further box has opened requesting information about how much data to import. By selecting **OK** you can preview the data in the file. If it is suitable a further **OK** may open the Import Options box, which gives you control over imported style names. Selecting **OK** will then open the file and place the selected contents in an 'Untitled' Ami Pro document.

If you select **Insert**, instead of **OK**, the imported data will be placed at the cursor location of the current document.

Importing into Tables:

If you insert a text file into a table, Ami Pro will place the entire file into the current table cell. However if you insert a data file into a table, Ami Pro places the data into the appropriate cells, and if you insert a data file into an empty selected frame, Ami Pro creates and places the data into a table with the correct number of columns and rows.

Importing and Exporting ASCII Files:

When you select ASCII as the file format, you should select the **ASCII Options** button, to open this dialogue box. Selecting **CR/LF at lines** causes file lines to be combined into paragraphs. Choose this option if the ASCII file is formatted with a Carriage Return/Line Feed at the end of every line and two Carriage Returns/ Line Feeds at the end of every paragraph.

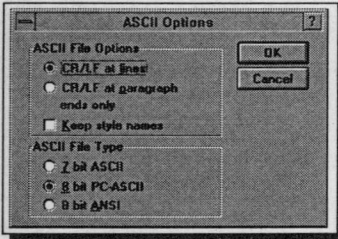

CR/LF at paragraph ends only causes each line to be imported as a separate paragraph. You select this option if the ASCII file is formatted with a Carriage Return/Line Feed at the end of each paragraph.

The **Keep style names** option allows you to import an ASCII file in which you have embedded style names for each paragraph. Each paragraph in the file should be preceded by the paragraph style name enclosed in angle brackets, '< >'. This will, of course, only work if the style names in the document are recognised by Ami Pro; otherwise the 'Body Text' style will be used.

Finally one of the following **ASCII File Types** must be selected to guarantee a successful operation. You may need to experiment here to get the best results.

7 bit ASCII if the character set used in the file contains only the first 128 characters of the IBM PC-ASCII character set.

140

8 bit PC-ASCII if your files were created in, or are to be used in a non-Windows application. This character set contains characters from the complete IBM set, including Greek and math symbols and foreign accented characters.

8 bit ANSI if your files were created in, or are to be used in, a Windows application. With this option Ami Pro imports, or exports, all the Windows ANSI characters.

Exporting Files:

To export a file in another application format you use the **File**, **Save As** command, which as we have seen before opens the following dialogue box.

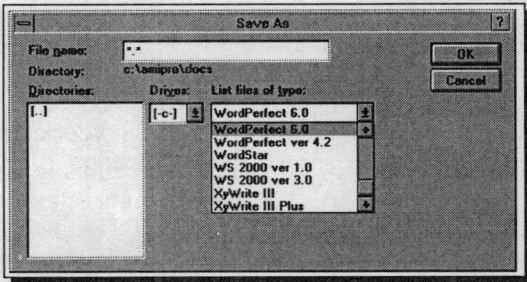

Open the **List files of type** window and the four normal option choices below disappear. Select the required document format and select **OK** to export.

With ASCII files you are given the same ASCII file type options as described previously. If you export to an ASCII format the current document from which you are exporting will also be converted to an ASCII document. This can cause confusion if you do not expect it. Obviously you should save it normally before the export operation, if you want to keep a copy of the document in Ami Pro format. You would most likely need this facility to produce, or edit, MS-DOS batch files or source text for a programming package like Microsoft QuickBASIC.

Revision Marking

You can use Revision Marking to keep track of any insertions and deletions you make to a document while it is being revised. Revision Marking also keeps track of any columns and rows you add or delete in a table, and any frames you insert or delete, (but not any changes you make to frames or paragraph styles).

You enable Revision Marking mode for each document you want to edit with the **Tools**, **Revision Marking** command and selecting the **Mark revisions** option, or by clicking the Typing Mode button on the status bar until Rev is displayed. Ami Pro will then automatically mark insertions and deletions as you make them. When you finish editing a document, you can review, accept, or cancel the revisions in the same box shown here, which is opened with the **Tools**, **Revision Marking** command.

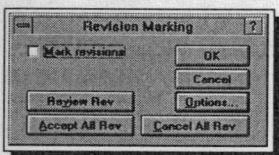

Selecting **Options** from this box gives you control over how insertions and deletions are displayed in your document. The options shown below are the default settings.

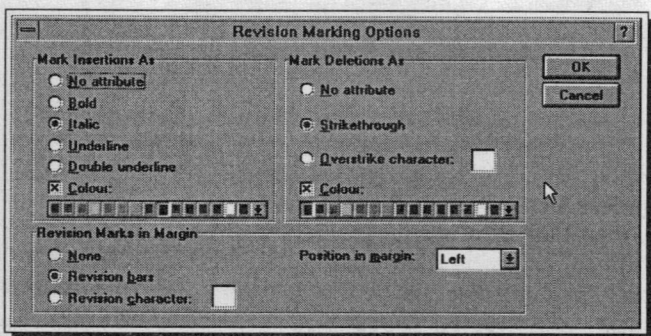

12. AMI PRO MACRO BASICS

Ami Pro Macros

A macro is simply a set of instructions made up of a sequence of keystrokes, mouse selections, or of commands stored in a macro file. After saving, or writing, a macro and attaching a quick key combination, or SmartIcon, to it, you can run the same sequence of commands whenever you want. This can save a lot of time and, especially with repetitive operations, can save mistakes creeping into your work.

In Ami Pro there are three basic ways of creating macros. The first two are generated by the program saving a series of keystrokes, or mouse clicks. The simplest, a 'Quick' macro, is used for short 'one off' tasks. Quick macros are not named and in fact you can only have one of these saved at any time.

The next type is created in the same manner, but the macros are named and saved in a macro directory. This type can be used repetitively.

For programming buffs, Ami Pro comes with a very comprehensive Macro Programming Language. You can write quite complex macro programs directly into a macro file and let Ami Pro compile them for you.

Recording a Macro:

To demonstrate how easy it is to save and name a macro, we will start with a simplistic one that enhances the word at the cursor to bold type in italics. Place the cursor in a document word and select **Tools**, **Macros**, **Record**, which opens the dialogue box shown here.

Type a name for your macro (call it firstmac) in the **Macro file** window, and a suitable key stroke combination in the **Playback shortcut keys** window.

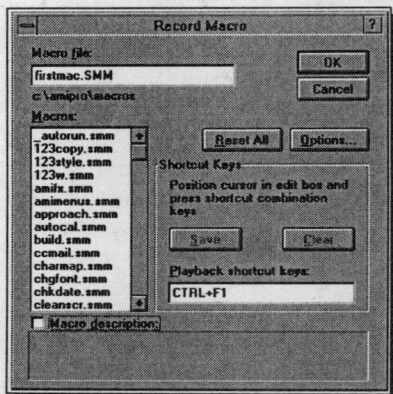

Most combinations of the <Ctrl> or <Shift> keys with a function key are suitable. The example shown uses <Ctrl+F1>. If the combination chosen is already used by Ami Pro you will be warned.

As you can see in the **Macros** window, Ami Pro macros have the file extension '.SMM' and are stored in a subdirectory of the program. When you have finished in this box click on **OK**. You will be returned to your editing screen, but a red message 'Recording Macro' will be placed on the status bar. While that message is active, all key strokes and mouse clicks (but not mouse movements in the editing area) will be recorded.

While the cursor is still placed in the word to be modified, use the key strokes, <Ctrl+→> followed by <Shift+Ctrl+←>, to highlight the word, then select **Bold** and **Italic**, either from the **Text** menu, or by clicking their SmartIcons. Press <Esc>, to cancel the highlight and stop recording by clicking your mouse on the red status bar message. Your macro should now be recorded and saved.

Playing Back a Macro:

There are three main ways of activating a macro. You can use the playback shortcut keys straight from the keyboard. In our case place the cursor in another word and press <Ctrl+F1>. The word should be enhanced automatically. If not check back that you carried out the instructions.

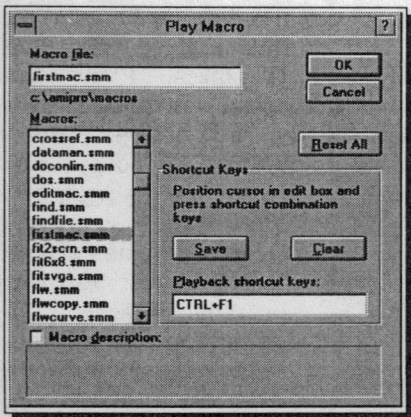

The second method is to select **Tools**, **Macros**, **Playback** from the menu bar. You can then select your macro name from the **Macros** window of the 'Play Macro' box, as shown here. The last method is to attach the macro to a custom SmartIcon, and simply click it. We will describe this process later in the chapter.

Quick Macros:

To save the bother of naming and retrieving a short temporary macro, you can use the **Tools**, **Macros**, **Quick Record** command, which puts you straight into recording mode. You record the macro in the same way as described above, and activate it with the **Tools**, **Macros**, **Quick Playback** command.

An even better procedure is to select shortcut key strokes for both the **Quick Record** and the **Quick Playback** actions, by selecting **Options** in the 'Record Macro' dialogue box.

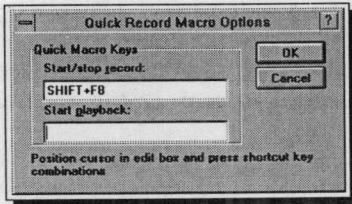

Enter your start and stop quick keys in the two windows. In the box here the entry <Shift+F8> is shown for the **Start/stop record** option. You might choose <Ctrl+F8> in the **Start playback** window, which would make it an easy key combination to remember. This procedure only needs doing once, unless of course you want to change the quick keys. To activate any quick macro in the future you would simply have to press the <Ctrl+F8> key combination.

Yet another way of activating a quick macro is to install the 'Playback a quick macro' SmartIcon on your Icon palette (Icon bar), and simply click on it when you need the macro action.

Editing a Macro:

You can edit the entries in a macro file by selecting the **Tools**, **Macros**, **Edit** command which opens yet another dialogue box in which you select the macro file to edit, or make changes to the shortcut keys selected. Open the 'firstmac.smm' file in this way, assuming of course that you saved it with that name. Ami Pro loads the file into the normal editing screen and you treat the macro file exactly the same as any other. The contents will probably· look like the following listing.

```
FUNCTION FIRSTMAC1()
Type( "[CTRLRight][CTRLSHIFTLeft]" )
Bold( )
Italic( )
Type( "[Esc]" )
END FUNCTION
```

If you look at this listing you will see that it would be very easy to edit the commands in the file. If you do edit it, you should then save the file in the normal way. You could also have opened the file yourself with **File**, **Open**, but using the **Macro Edit** procedure saved you having to bother with a different directory or file extension.

The Macro Programming Language

We do not have the time or space in this publication to cover the Ami Pro macro language, but if you need it, help is not very far away. Choose **Help**, **Macro Doc**, to open the on-line macro documentation, shown below.

You can get involved with macro programming if you are that way inclined, but we have included just a short routine to

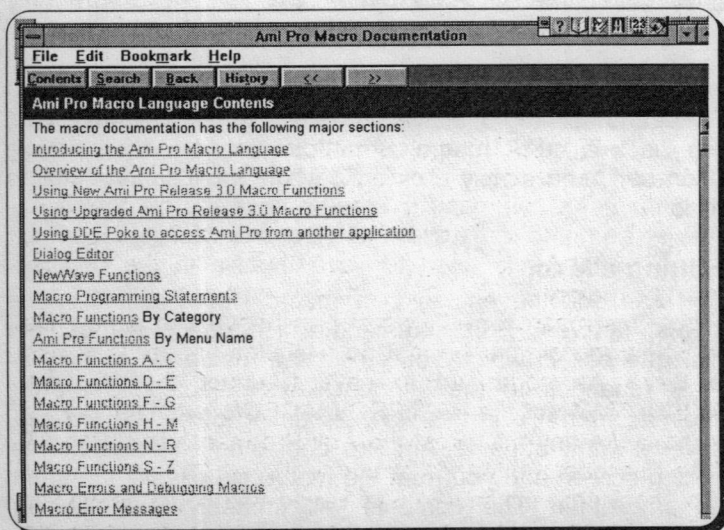

show the flavour of the language which, in fact, is not far removed from Basic.

The macro 'save2A' was written to help with our day to day use of Ami Pro. Whenever the office computer is finished with for the day, the current working file is copied to a floppy disc, both for back up and to transport home for evening, or weekend work. This macro copies the active file to the A: drive.

A Sample Macro Program:

```
FUNCTION SAVE2A()
DEFSTR Char;
CurDir=GetCurrentDir$()
OpenFile = GetOpenFileName$()
I = len(OpenFile)
WHILE "\" != Assign(&Char,
MID$(OpenFile, I, 1))
I = I - 1
WEND
FileName = Right$(OpenFile,
(len(OpenFile) - I))
SaveAs("A:\{FileName}" 0 "" "" )
SaveAs("{CurDir}{FileName}" 0 "" "" )
END FUNCTION
```

This may not be the most elegant solution, but it works. The open file (with full path) and current directory are assigned to variables. The file name is extracted from the full path details and a **Save As** command is used to save the file to the A: drive. So as not to leave the A: drive as the working location, another **Save As** is used to save the file in the original working directory.

Type this macro exactly as shown above into a new file and when you are happy that no mistakes appear in it, use the **Save As** command to save it under the filename **SAVE2A.SMM** in the \AMIPRO\MACROS subdirectory. If you do make any mistakes, the Ami Pro macro compiler will refuse to accept the file. So be warned!

To check that the macro was saved you could select the **Tools**, **Macros**, **Edit** command and look for its name in the

Macros window. You could also assign a quick key combination to it in the same dialogue box.

Linking to a SmartIcon

To get the full use out of the macro facility you need to link your most often used macros to icons that can be easily accessed from your SmartIcon palettes.

This is done from the **SmartIcons** dialogue box which is accessed by selecting it from the **Tools** menu. When initially opened, the box will look like the example below. The left window lists the icons which are available to your system.

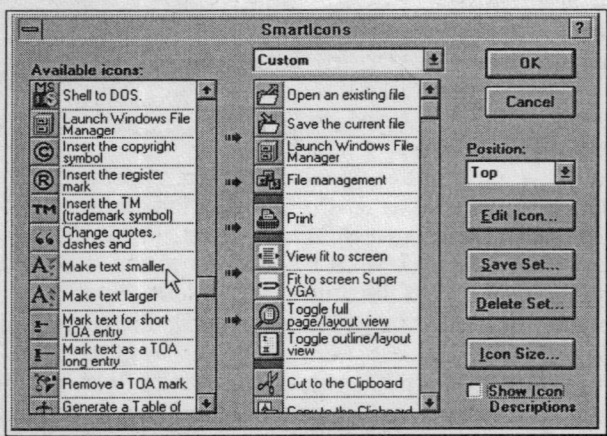

The right window shows the icons that are placed in the palette named in the top window.

At the moment we want to design a new icon for our macro. The easy way to do this is to edit the design of an existing one. The nearest to our needs is the one shown above as 'Make text smaller'. Click on this icon in the 'Available icons' window and select **Edit Icon** to open the icon designer screen shown on the next page.

Before doing anything else, select **Save As** to open an icon file for you to edit. Otherwise you may spoil the Ami Pro custom icon selected. Name the new SmartIcon 'Save2A', so

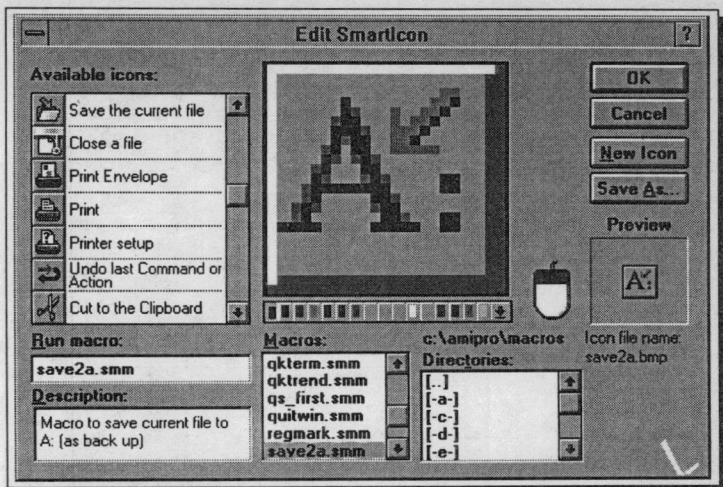

Edit SmartIcon

Available icons:
- Save the current file
- Close a file
- Print Envelope
- Print
- Printer setup
- Undo last Command or Action
- Cut to the Clipboard

OK
Cancel
New Icon
Save As...

Preview

Run macro:
save2a.smm

Description:
Macro to save current file to A: (as back up)

Macros:
qkterm.smm
qktrend.smm
qs_first.smm
quitwin.smm
regmark.smm
save2a.smm

c:\amipro\macros
Directories:
[..]
[-a-]
[-c-]
[-d-]
[-e-]

Icon file name:
save2a.bmp

that it will always be obvious which macro it partners. All you have to do now is change the icon in the centre window. Click the mouse on the colour you want, in the colour bar below it. Whenever you click the mouse in the edit window that pixel will change to the selected colour. Have fun. The **Preview** to the right of the centre window shows you what your icon will look like at its normal size.

When you have finished, save your design with the **Save As** button and select 'save2a.smm' in the **Macros** window, to link your icon to that macro. The entries in the **Run macro** and **Description** windows will be placed automatically, as long as you entered a file description when you first saved the macro file. Select **OK** to return to the 'SmartIcons' box and check that your icon is at the end of the 'Available icons' list as shown overleaf.

Customising a SmartIcon Palette:
Ami Pro comes with 10 SmartIcon palettes to choose from. After using the program for a while you will know which icons you use most and would best be placed together. To include a new icon on a palette, select which existing icon palette is nearest to the custom design you want, and click on **Save**

SmartIcons ?

Available icons: Custom ▼

Exit from Windows   Open an existing file
Find and open documents   Save the current file
Macro to save current file to A: (as back up)   A: Macro to save current file to A: (as back up)
                                    Launch Windows File Manager
                                    File management
                                    Print
                                    View fit to screen
                                    Fit to screen Super VGA
                                    Toggle full page/layout view
                                    Toggle outline/layout view
                                    Cut to the Clipboard

OK
Cancel

Position:
Top ▼

Edit Icon...
Save Set...
Delete Set...
Icon Size...

☐ Show Icon Descriptions

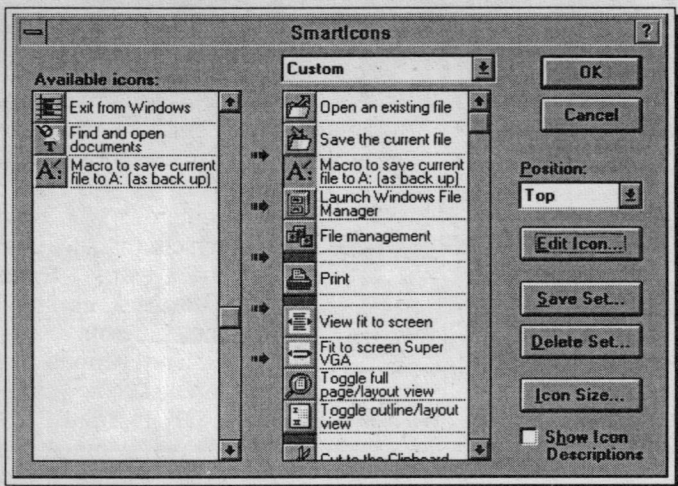

Set to open a new set. Enter whatever name you want and you are ready to modify the icons in the new set.

To remove an icon from your set, drag it out of the right window and release the mouse button. To add an icon, drag it from the left window of 'Available icons' into your icon set and release it on the existing icon you want it to be in front of. It will 'push' its way in. You can also reposition icons on your palette set in the same way. When you are finished, select **Save Set** and then **OK**. Your new set should be available to you when you click on the SmartIcon button on the status bar.

SmartIcon Help Messages:

A new addition to the SmartIcon dialogue box with Ami Pro 3.1 is the option to **Show Icon Descriptions**, located in the bottom right hand corner. Clearing this selection will disable the annoying yellow bubble Icon descriptions, which otherwise appear whenever your mouse pointer moves over the SmartIcon bar in the main screen. You can still see the bubbles if you right click your mouse on an icon.

Customising Ami Pro

As you have seen in this chapter, Ami Pro comes with a large selection of ready-made macros, which are listed in the **Macros** windows of the 'Macro' dialogue boxes.

To find out what these do and to customise the package by setting some to run automatically whenever Ami Pro is opened, run the macro 'specialf.smm', as described earlier. This is the 'Special features' macro, which initially places the extra **Special Features** choice on the **Tools** menu which opens the small box shown here. The first time, you should select **OK** to read the file 'goodies.sam', as this describes all the available macros and the options available to you. Then select **Install special features** which will let you select which macros you want to 'Autorun' whenever Ami Pro starts. By this stage you should be quite happy finding your own way round this procedure.

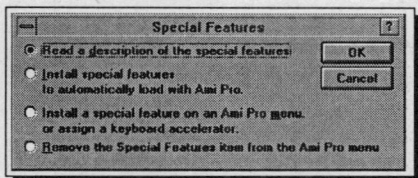

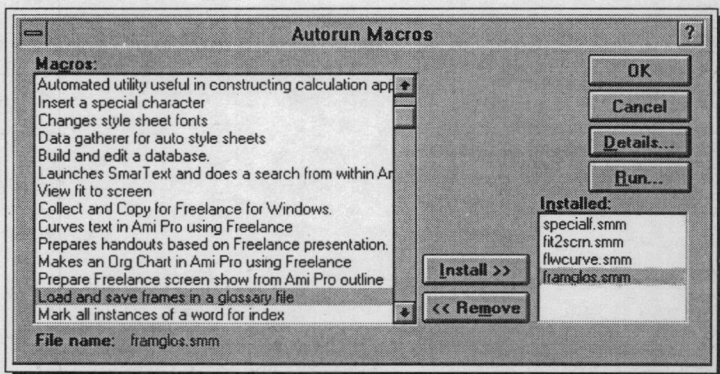

APPENDIX A
KEYBOARD SHORTCUTS

Shortcuts for Menu Commands:

To perform this action	*Press this*
Access Styles Box	Ctrl+Y
Bold text	Ctrl+B
Centre text	Ctrl+E
Copy	Ctrl+Ins or Ctrl+C
Cut	Shift+Del or Ctrl+X
Delete next word	Ctrl+Del
Delete previous word	Ctrl+BkSp
Draft/layout view	Ctrl+M
Fast Format	Ctrl+T
Find & Replace	Ctrl+F
Full page/previous layout view	Ctrl+D
Go To	Ctrl+G
Go To next item	Ctrl+H
Insert glossary record	Ctrl+K
Italicise text	Ctrl+I
Justify text	Ctrl+J
Left align text	Ctrl+L
Modify a paragraph style	Ctrl+A
Normal text	Ctrl+N
Open document	Ctrl+O
Paste	Shift+Ins or Ctrl+V
Print document	Ctrl+P
Right align text	Ctrl+R
Save	Ctrl+S
Show/Hide set of SmartIcons	Ctrl+Q
Underline text	Ctrl+U
Undo previous action	Alt+BkSp or Ctrl+Z
Word underline text	Ctrl+W

Shortcuts for Navigating and Selecting Text:

To move or select	Press this
Left one character	←
Right one character	→
Up one line	↑
Down one line	↓
Left one word	Ctrl+←
Right one word	Ctrl+→
Beginning of line	Home
End of line	End
Previous sentence	, (comma)
Next sentence	Ctrl+. (full stop)
Paragraph beginning	Ctrl+↑
Paragraph end	Ctrl+↓
Up one screen	PgUp
Down one screen	PgDn
Top of previous page	Ctrl+PgUp
Top of next page	Ctrl+PgDn
To beginning of file	Ctrl+Home
To end of file	Ctrl+End

Shortcuts in Outline Mode:

To perform this action	Press this
To contract a paragraph	Alt+PgUp
To expand a paragraph	Alt+PgDn
To contract a document	Alt+1
To expand a document	Alt+0
To expand a level (n)	Alt+n
To move paragraph up	Alt+↑
To move paragraph down	Alt+↓
To promote paragraph	Alt+←
To demote paragraph	Alt+→

APPENDIX B
AMI PRO SMARTICONS

File Menu SmartIcons:

Create a new file

Open an existing file

Close a file

Save the current file

Import a picture

File Management

Send Mail

Merge

Print envelope

Print

Printer set-up

Exit Ami Pro

Edit Menu SmartIcons:

Undo last command or action

Cut to Clipboard

Copy to Clipboard

Paste Clipboard contents

155

	Find & Replace
	Go To
	Insert bullet
	Insert date/time
	Insert today's date
	Insert note
	Insert glossary record
	Insert power fields
	Update selected power fields
	Update all power fields
	Go To next power field
	Go To previous power field
	Insert index mark
	No hyphenation
	Bookmarks
	Delete

View Menu SmartIcons:

	Toggle full page/previous layout view
	Toggle outline/layout view

	Toggle draft/layout view
	Show/Hide ruler
	Show/Hide clean screen
	Show/Hide power fields
	Show/Hide column guides
	Show/Hide margins in colour
	Show/Hide pictures
	Show/Hide tabs & returns
	Show/Hide marks
	Show/Hide notes
	Show/Hide vertical ruler
	View Preferences

Text Menu SmartIcons:

	Change font, point size, and colour of text
	Left align selected text
	Centre selected text
	Right align selected text
	Justify selected text
	Indent all lines of paragraph
	Indent first line of paragraph

▤	Indent all but first line of paragraph
N	Normal text
B	Bold text
I	Italicise text
U	Underline text
U	Word underline text
aA	Capitalise text
Abc	Capitalise first letter of each word
S^s	Superscript text
S$_s$	Subscript Text
U	Double underline text
✎	Fast Format On

Style Menu SmartIcons:

▨	Modify a paragraph style
S	Define a paragraph style

Page Menu SmartIcons:

▤	Insert a header/footer
▤	Modify page layout
▤1	Insert a page number

	Insert a page break

Frame Menu SmartIcons:

	Add a frame
	Add a frame using previous size and position settings
	Modify frame layout
	Scale a picture
	Toggle group/ungroup frames
	Bring frame to front
	Send frame to back

Tools Menu SmartIcons:

	Spell Check
	Grammar Check
	Thesaurus
	Create a table
	Create a drawing
	Charting
	Equations
	Insert footnote

159

Revision marking

Document compare

Sort in ascending order

Generate TOC, Index

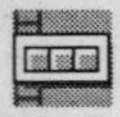

Floating SmartIcons

Customise SmartIcons

Switch SmartIcon sets

Start/stop recording a quick macro

Play back a quick macro

Toggle start/stop recording a macro

Play back a macro

Table Menu SmartIcons:

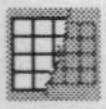

Modify table layout

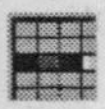

Modify lines & colours

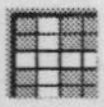

Insert column or row

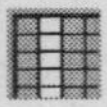

Insert column after current column

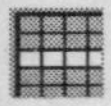

Insert row after current row

Delete column or row

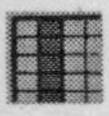

Delete selected columns

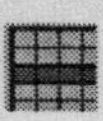

Delete selected rows

Delete an entire table

Size columns & rows

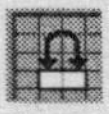

Connect selected cells

Edit formula

Window Menu SmartIcons:

Tile windows

Cascade windows

Help Menu SmartIcons:

Quick Start Tutorial

Custom Macro SmartIcons:

Details on some of these are included in the sample files placed in the default document directory during installation.

Launch 1-2-3 for Windows

Launch Lotus Freelance for Windows

Launch Lotus SmarText

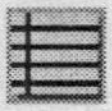

Load Lotus Notes

Launch Lotus cc:Mail

Launch Lotus Approach

Launch Lotus Organiser

Quick access to Lotus SmartPics

Shell to DOS

Launch Windows File Manager

Insert copyright symbol

Insert register mark

Insert trademark symbol

Change quotes and dashes

Make text smaller

Make text larger

Mark text for short TOA entry

Mark text for long TOA entry

Remove a TOA mark

Generate a table of Authorities

View fit to screen

Select pages to print

Print the current document with defaults

Autorun multiple macros

Build and edit a database

Select multiple files to print

Print the selected text

Centre frame to page

Set frame to page layout

Load and save frames in a glossary

Find and open documents

Create new file with default style sheet

Close all open documents

Select multiple documents to open

Save selected text to a new file

Save with Doc Info

Locate files by Doc Info

Tile horizontally open documents

Customise Ami Pro menus

Macro MindBlaster game

Collect and copy info from 123 for Windows

Create Ami Pro styles in 123 for Windows

Calculation application builder

Launches SmarText to carry out search

Collect and copy for Freelance for Windows

Curves text in Ami Pro from Freelance

Prepares handouts from a Freelance presentation

Makes an Organisation chart from Freelance

Prepare Freelance show from Ami Pro outline

Collect and copy info from Improv

Lotus Application Manager

Tile Lotus applications

Create a calendar from Organiser data

Calculate a depreciation schedule

Return value of a formula or @ function

Calculate sine, cosine or tangent of an angle

Calculate percentages of a series of numbers

Calculate a number raised to a power

Calculate real solutions for a quadratic equation

Calculate the root of a number

Calculate savings from regular monthly amount

Compose Lotus Mail Messages in Ami Pro

Calculate basic numeric summary information

Calculate loan payment

Convert temperatures between °F and °C

Calculate time period for equal deposits

INDEX

NOTES

COMPANION DISC TO THIS BOOK

This book contains many pages of file/program listings. There is no reason why you should spend hours typing them into your computer, unless you wish to do so, or need the practice.

The COMPANION DISC for this book comes with all the example listings. It is available in both 3.5-inch and 5.25-inch formats.

COMPANION DISCS for all books written by the same author(s) and published by BERNARD BABANI (publishing) LTD, are also available and are listed at the front of this book. Make sure you fill in your name and address and specify the book number, title and the disc size in your order.

ORDERING INSTRUCTIONS

To obtain your copy of the companion disc, fill-in the order form below, enclose a cheque (payable to **P.R.M. Oliver**) or a postal order, and send it to the address given below.

Book No.	Book Name	Unit Price	Total Price
BP		£3.50	
BP		£3.50	
BP		£3.50	
Name .... Address		Sub-total	£.............
		P & P (@ 45p/disc)	£.............
Disc Format 3.5-inch....... 5.25-inch......		Total Due	£.............

Send to: P.R.M. Oliver, CSM, Pool, Redruth, Cornwall, TR15 3SE